WORK HEALTH AND SAFETY MANAGEMENT IN THE AUSTRALIAN STATES

By Tim Damianidis

Work Health and Safety Management in The Australian States

This eBook was published in 2024 by

Tim Damianidis

Hillarys WA, 6025

1st Edition

Revision 1.03

DIGITAL EBOOK, ISBN-13: 978-1-7637431-0-6

PAPERBACK, ISBN-13: 978-1-7637431-1-3

HARDCOVER, ISBN-13: 978-1-7637431-2-0

Dedication

To Stavros

Abstract

This book provides a refreshing new look at WHS management systems. It takes the reader on a journey through the Australian States and their legal framework. It explores common legal terms used in Australia. Then refreshingly looks at a Statistical model that encapsulates the records and statistics that a mature organisation would require. Following these introductory elements the Health and Safety system, using ISO45001 structure is explored. The exploration utilises the latest in academic papers and practical knowledge and experience gained over decades. In addition, some noteworthy components are also covered such as issue resolution, consultation processes and emergency planning. Overall, *"Work Health and Safety Management in the Australian States"* is a must-read for any WHS professional working in Australia.

Prologue

A significant portion of the current economic climate ranging from 2008 till the time of writing this book, has seen the micro business in Australia close down in significant proportions.

Table A

Number of businesses entering and exiting the market between 2020-24

Year	Entries	Exits	Net
2020-21	365,480	-277,674	87,806
2021-22	442,555	-305,085	137,470
2022-23	406,365	-356,216	50,149
2023-24	436,018	-362,893	73,125

(Australian Bureau of Statistics, 2024)

There was a spike during COVID-19 times as many scrambled to try and save their finances by opening businesses. Many faced unemployment and had little in terms of options other than to become self-employed.

Figure 1. *The net number of businesses surviving each year between 2020-24*

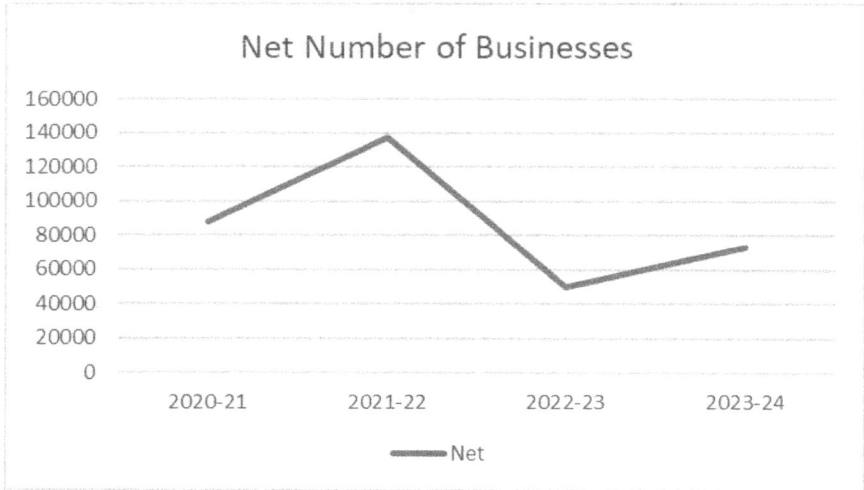

The landscape is still dominated by many small businesses in terms of numbers. Keep in mind that small businesses include those large franchise companies that operate based on leasing a business model, trademark and logo. Many small independent micro shops have closed around Australia (Australian Bureau of Statistics, 2024; Clark et al., 2011).

Adding to the demise of small independent businesses is the pressure from the new legislation. The work health and safety laws have become more punitive in recent years (*Model Work Health and Safety Act 2011*, Austl.; *Model Work Health and Safety Regulations 2011*, Austl.). Perhaps the large increase from tens of thousands to hundreds of thousands in penalties has some merit, but for the most part, it is a deterrent to small operators who are unlikely to be completely compliant.

For the most part, the new WHS laws coupled with the new ISO 45001 Standard, all have a major impact on the tapestry of the business world. Many of the business models have slowly begun to disappear and instead, there is an emerging system that mimics government. These systems are called mature machines. Others call it communism or socialism.

Overall, we can say that the standard of safety and health has been given a new and higher bar to measure against. A more complete and robust system that aligns globally. However, it is not without shortcomings.

Having worked in small, medium and large enterprises, I know for a fact that what works in one business environment doesn't work in another. This is why much of the global agenda is attempting to regulate how business is done. The dynamic foray of small business models is slowly shaping them into ill-equipped bureaucratic models based on the mature machine organisational context. Governance in these businesses has shifted from Autocratic models to Oligarchical and for the most part, external undocumented factors influence the business internally and significantly.

A sincere attempt to remain neutral has been applied to this book. It should be noted that the purpose of it is to help all businesses meet their obligations. The aim was to help businesses from small independent fast food sole traders to the multi-national multi-site organisation. Therefore, what follows is a sincere look at how WHS can be done and it takes into account some of those older and unique business models we rarely see today.

Contents

xiii

Further Reading

Australian Bureau of Statistics. (2024). *Counts of Australian Businesses, including Entries and Exits.* https://www.abs.gov.au/statistics/economy/business-indicators/counts-australian-businesses-including-entries-and-exits/latest-release.

Clark, M., Eaton, M., Lind, W., Pye, E., & Bateman, L. (2011). *Key Statistics - Small Business Publication.* Commonwealth of Australia. https://treasury.gov.au/sites/default/files/2019-03/SmallBusinessPublication.pdf

Model Work Health and Safety Act 2011. (Austl.).

Model Work Health and Safety Regulations 2011. (Austl.).

Introduction

Thousands of people perish due to workplace incidents every year in Australia. Also, hundreds of thousands are injured in the workplace around Australia. Progressively, people are being injured less each year between 2005-2022. In comparison, there were approximately 663,000 injuries in 2005 at workplaces throughout Australia. In 2022 there were approximately 497,000 injuries at work (Australian Bureau Of Statistics, 2023). It would be fair to estimate that millions of hazards have been identified and treated but not as many as could be. In 2023, New South Wales (NSW) with 60 fatalities, Queensland (Qld) with 51 fatalities and Western Australia (WA) with 27 fatalities had the highest death count. However, concerning per capita of workers; SA (1.8/100,000) and Northern Territory (NT) (3.6/100,000) were the worst performers. Tasmania (Tas) was the best performer.

The type of industries undertaken in Queensland and Western Australia are overrepresented by resource operations. Western Australia is the epicentre for mining in Australia. NSW has a very large construction industry, possibly accounting for the higher occurrence of fatal incidents. Health care is the largest industry in NSW and could also contribute significantly to the number of non-fatal

1

injuries. Queensland like Western Australia has a large mining and construction sector.

Figure 2. *Deaths and injuries in the Australian states*

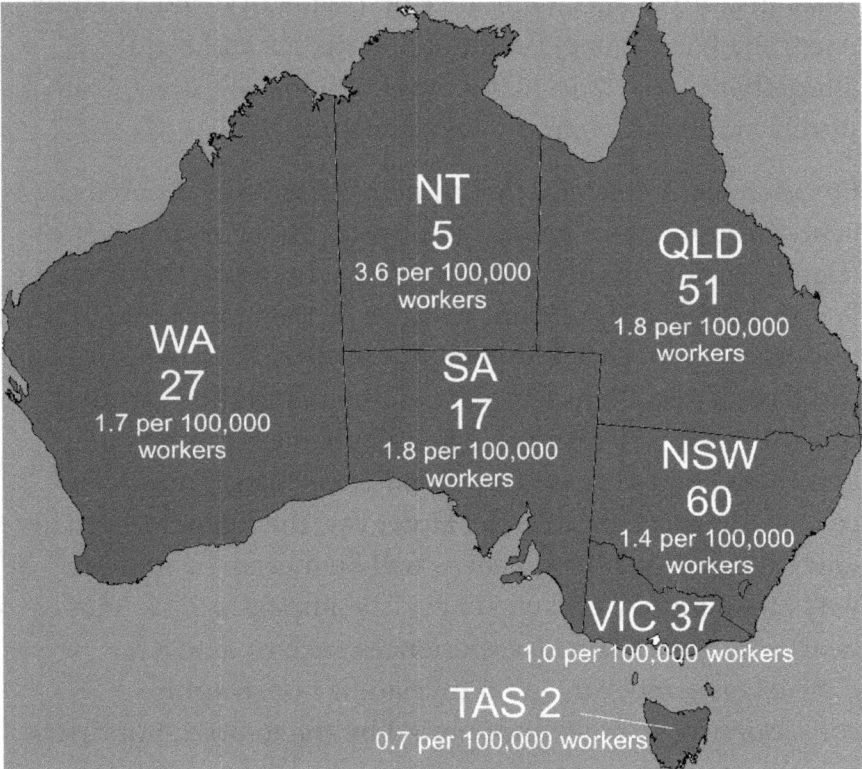

(As at Sept 2024, adapted from Australian Bureau Of
Statistics, 2023; Safe Work Australia, 2024b)

Note: Fatality counts are per entire population. However,
incident rates are given per 100,000 employees and indicate
the location of where the incidents happened not their
jurisdiction.

The problem, if not immediately obvious by the statistics, will be defined by the human aspects of the predicament. Also, in comparison with other first-world Western nations, Australia has similar comparable statistics and is not altogether worse than many other nations. We can't, from a purely statistical point of view, conclude.

For each work-related fatality, major and huge repercussions echo through entire groups of people. The workplace, the friends' group, family and everyone who knew the deceased is impacted in a significant manner. Some mourn and others undergo psychosocial impact that is difficult to measure but can have a detrimental impact on them and those around them. It is all well and good to talk business talk to the employer such as downtime, insurance costs, uninsured costs, workplace morale etc. However, the impact internally and externally on the business will be measured in more ways than money and currency. The impact will be tears, heartache, psychosocial experiences such as anxiety, distrust, absenteeism and a myriad of catastrophic consequences when compounded by the tenfold, hundreds and thousands of people impacted by such an incident.

Work health and safety also known as occupational health and safety, has a simple task. To limit the risk of harm to people through those that introduce risks through their work. However, this should not deter the people working towards a particular standard or from aspiring to do the absolute good and pinnacle good. That is to say that minimising the risks is only one step in providing workplaces with a positive and beneficial experience. Some call striving for excellence an unrealistic ideal, yet most strive for the highest possible goals.

This book will now discuss issues mainly to do with Australia. There may be some references and perhaps the inclusion of foreign information if it serves a particular use to the information presented. The book contains a discussion of the Australian States and their legal framework including common legal terms and matters. Following this, a statistical model is established to assist managers in developing their management systems. Risk management, safety and health management and quality management are also addressed. Then there is a look at some legal entities that need to be a part of the system, consultative systems dispute resolution, incident response, emergency response and people management.

The History of WHS

The Code of Hammurabi has multiple punitive actions against unsafe construction, including homes and ships. "If a builder builds a house for a man and do not make its construction firm, and the house which he has built collapse and cause the death of the owner of the house, that builder shall be put to death (Hammurabi, 1792 BC, s.229-233). Also, "If a boatman build a boat for a man and he do not make its construction seaworthy and that boat meets with a disaster in the same year in which it was put into commission, the boatman shall reconstruct that boat and he shall strengthen it at his own expense and he shall give the boat when strengthened to the owner of the boat" (Hammurabi, 1792 BC, s.235).

According to Herodotus , around 600BC-500BC a military called Cnidians or Knidians began digging a trench to create an island out of a land that had an isthmus joining it to the mainland. In one of the translations it reads; "Many of them were at this work; and seeing that the workers were injured when breaking stones more often and less naturally than usual, some in other ways, but most in the eyes, the Cnidians sent envoys to Delphi to inquire what it was that opposed them" (Herodotus, 450BC; 1920, s.1.174).

It wasn't the first time large teams had been commissioned to work on large projects using advanced machinery and natural strength. However, Herodotus documents two things, while it was possible to complete the works it was seen as unethical because of their religious convictions. Secondly, the process was considered unsafe. Safety had started to become an issue as technology and organised labour emerged.

During the Renaissance, 1556 AD, Georgius Agricola writes about miners' health issues including pestilence, ventilation and ergonomics. Agricola in translation states "…a wise miner does not mine in such places, even if they are very productive, when he perceives unmistakable' signs of pestilence. For if a man mines in an unhealthy region he may be alive one hour and dead the next"(Agricola, 1556).

Paracelsus the father of toxicology similarly writes about miners' health issues but claims all things can be poisonous based on the dose. "If you wish justly to explain each poison, what is there that is not poison? All things are poison, and nothing is without poison: the Dosis alone makes a thing not poison. For example, every food and every drink, if taken beyond its Dose, is poison: the result proves it"(Paracelsus, 1541, p. 22).

Then as the industrial age emerged Bernardini Ramazzini published his works "De Morbis Artificum Diatribe", or in English; "The Diseases of Workers". It was a comprehensive coverage of occupational diseases. Overall the concerns for occupational diseases, injuries and wellbeing had become more apparent as the industrial age began to emerge (Ramazzini, 1700).

As the self-determination of the people diminished under Oligarchical rule, the proportion of the population compelled to work increased. Exact figures are difficult to determine and compare, however from 1700-1800 the consensus is that agricultural work and self-employment were the main ways of life. The economic policies of that time, called Mercantilism, promoted local production and encouraged exports. This in turn promoted local agriculture as the most common form of export. The bulk of the technology was still in simple human or animal-driven technologies like hand drills, ox or horse-driven ploughs, donkey or mule-driven mills etc. However, by the mid-1700s, the technology of steam-powered engines and other factory and workshop machinery began to emerge. Women and children made up a large proportion of the employed population. Instead of a single person tending to a farm with the help of his family, the women and children were enticed to work in large workshops and factories. Over time the money made from these factories was higher than the farming income and a steady drop in agricultural business began to occur. From the 1800s onwards there is a steady increase in large work environments. The machinery had also become more complex. The level of employment by large companies increased hyperbolically. This is represented by a massive burst to the gross domestic product, especially between 1820 and 2020s. The Colonial period also known as the Autocratic period saw a dramatic increase in the demand for a higher GDP. Australia, Canada and many other British colonies contributed to a large share of the global GDP collectively.

An interesting point to make was that the GDP of Australia per capita was higher than Britain, and the United States of America and double that of Canada's (Greasley & Oxley, 1998). This turn of events, in human history, also brought significant changes into the workplace. Especially when the workforce was now concentrated in large business establishments in comparison to the small family-owned and operated ventures of the past. Unlike in the times of Herodotus's writings, the military culture had changed also. The organised labour introduced by military sourced, or prisoner of war sourced labour, had changed. The disciplined military workers were very different to the workforce that emerged during the Industrial Revolution between the 1700s to 1800's. From disciplined soldiers working on projects, the workforce became dominated by mainly undisciplined and lowly educated children. The females were also considered valuable workers. The men were the last to let go of their self-sufficiency on their farms and reluctantly followed when their agricultural incomes couldn't match that earned in factories. By the second Industrial Revolution from the 1800s to the modern era, there was an exponential growth of the industry as stated previously. Due to the initial employment of children and females by large companies, specific issues arose and hence serious issues derived from the work environment, impacted heavily on children.

Figure 3. *Gross domestic product (GDP) 1820 – 2022*

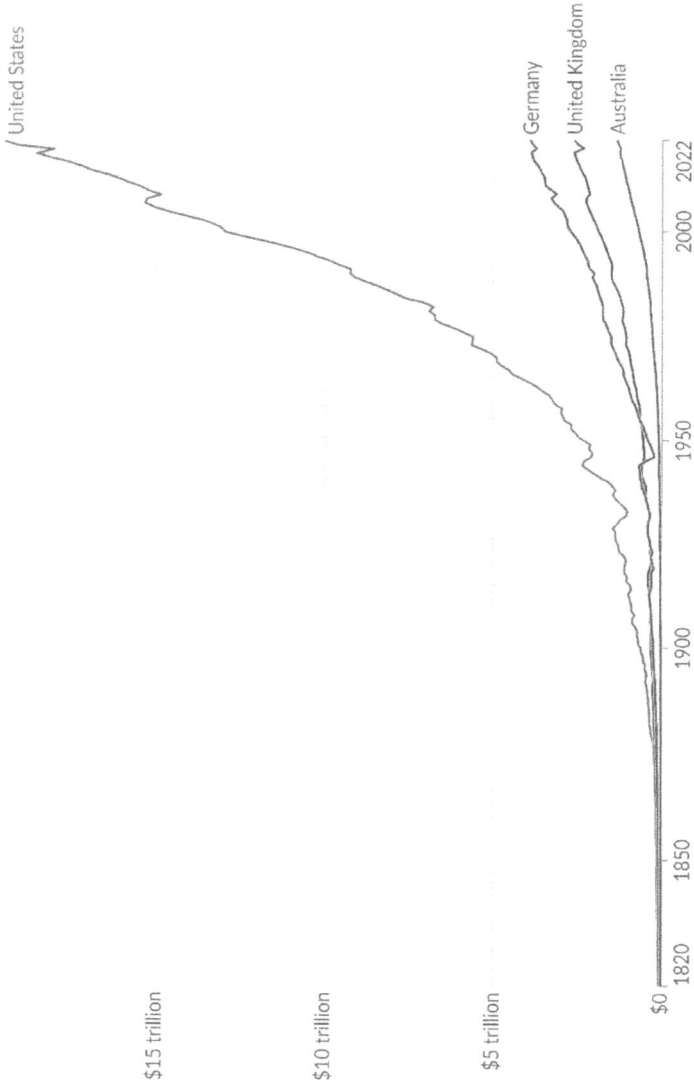

(Bolt & Zanden, 2024)

Introduction

Note: The data is expressed in international US dollars $ at 2011 prices. It is adjusted for inflation and differences in the cost of living between countries.

These historical developments led to a massive change in the industry demographics. Men, women and children were affected immensely by new technologies and ways of working. Although people had concerns for Safety and wrote many safety laws since ancient times, the new era they called the Industrial Age brought with it many reasons to put Safety and Health at the forefront of thought and occupation.

The Factory Acts

During the Industrial age and towards the modern era a number of industry changes were reflected by the laws of that era. In brief the following course of events led to the modern era of legislation. Please note that the UK legislation applied to the states of Australia where none existed. After the federation of the states, based on equal representation of the states, the law precedence and order changed. The State laws came first unless there was a Federated Commonwealth law. The judicature was fashioned similarly. However high court appeals were possible to escalate to UK courts throughout the history of Australia till the time of writing this.

Table 1

The Initial UK Action Against Workplace Injury

Year	Description	
1819	Peel Committee: Led by Sir Robert Peel.	Appointed by the House of Commons in the United Kingdom. Investigation into child labour.

Table 2

The Factory Acts of the UK

The UK Factory Acts		
Year	ACT Title	Description
1819	Act for the regulation of Cotton Mills and Factories Act 1819	Minimum employable age of 9 Children under 16 worked a maximum of 12-hour days.
1833	Factory Regulation Act	Included other factories aside cotton mills. Children 9-13 were educated at-least two hours a day. Salaried inspectors introduced Under 18-year-olds were forbidden from working night shifts or between 8:30pm and 8:30am 9–13-year-olds were allowed to work a maximum of 9-hour days 13–18-year-olds were allowed to work a maximum of 12-hour days
1844	Factory Amendment Act	Impacted the mining sector Had a regulations and Act format Minimum safety standards introduced for the first time Removed the *mens rea** clause that takes into account intention to act and the mental state of the accused.

1847	Factory Act	Reduced working hours for all ages to 10-hour days
1878	Factory and Workshops Act	Applied to more factories than before and not just factories but also workshops. It applied to all trades
1880	Employers Liability Act	Employee rights to compensation Removed *common employment defence*** against negligence. But did not fully remove the argument in other areas of law.

Notes: *Mens Rea – Contains three criteria; A person's knowledge that his conduct is criminal. Establishment of a criminal intent. A purpose or knowledge that is wrongfully involved with the incident.

****Common employment defence**, also known as the *fellow servant rule*, is a legal doctrine that historically protected employers from liability for injuries that employees sustained while at work if the injuries were caused by fellow employees.

Table 3

The Factory Acts of the Australian States

Australian Factory Acts		
Year	ACT Title	Description
1873	Supervision of Workrooms and Factories Statute (VIC.)	Following concerns for children the females were then considered a priority issue. Female work day limited to 8 hours per day
1885	Factories and Shops Act (VIC.)	A comprehensive act based on establishing a minimum set of work conditions.

Note: Similar acts came much later in the development of each State for example the Factories and Shops Act 1920 (W.A.) came later when W.A. began to develop its mining industry and city infrastructure.

Many other related laws were published during the period 1820-1984. The purpose here is to only highlight some key developments rather than a comprehensive list of legislation. By 1972 there were separate laws for mines, factories, agriculture, offices shops etc. Which all led to a need to consolidate, unify and rescope the purpose of the legislation. This was achieved by what became known as the Robens Report.

Robens' Report

Robens' Report is short for the Safety and Health at Work: report of the Committee, 1970-72. Robens' Report begins by identifying the problem and the purpose or scope of their investigation; "Our terms of reference invited us to consider whether any changes are needed in the scope or nature of the enactments dealing with occupational safety and health, in measures for protecting the public against hazards of industrial origin"(Robens, 1972, s.14). In s.27 of the report, it is summarised that the regulatory laws were inadequate and in dire need of change. One of the interesting points made was that the laws were too regulatory and relied on state enforcement or regulation. Instead, a system that encourages personal responsibility, and a voluntary, self-generating effort was proposed. Too many laws have been written in an attempt to remedy the same or similar situations found in all workplaces. There was a duty of care intruded on employers, designers and suppliers. Full-time permanent inspectors were recommended. Decriminalisation of injuries but criminalised wilful negligence and many more areas were recommended

- Management roles defined,
- Safety specialists or adviser roles defined,
- Workplace involvement,
- A consultation process must exist,
- Written health and safety policies,
- Company reports and risk or hazard reporting and treatment,
- Joint standing committees such as H&S committees,
- A request for unified legislation was also made

(Robens, 1972).

The report made some remarkable comments with great insight into the problems and the future developments of occupational safety and health. The committee had established the framework of the legislation that would soon follow. In 1974 the UK legislation Health and Safety at Work etc. Act 1974 included many of the recommendations and took on a similar framework to that proposed by the Robens' Report.

The response to occupational health and safety in the UK has impacted many countries including the USA, Canada, Australia and New Zealand. The UK legal developments sought to improve the administration and ethical application of moral Health and Safety in the workplace. Unfortunately, the scope was very different to its application. Every Australian State was a nominated legal jurisdiction and as such the diversity of laws remained existent. Each state had its laws as did the states of other countries like Canada. Most other countries had complex laws at the Federated or National level such as New Zealand, USA and South Africa. There remained some work to do to bring about a philosophically universal system.

Between 1974 and 2008 various places in the world adopted similar legislation, especially within the Anglosphere. These laws consolidated previous legislation and incorporated the new framework proposed by the Robens' Report.

Between 2008 and 2024 a series of changes and modifications occurred to develop a Globalist ideologically driven agenda. The intention was to harmonise and in effect globalise the occupational safety and health laws. The process began by establishing authoritative national bodies that would promote the development of unified law establishment. Then agreements were made between federal and state governments to achieve a unified outcome to align internally within Australia and externally with the Globalist driven Anglosphere.

Leading to Harmonised laws

The Council of Australian Governments (COAG) was the primary intergovernmental forum in Australia from 1992 to 2020. The Council of Australian Governments (COAG) in 2008 began the process of harmonizing the laws of occupational health and safety throughout Australia.

The process was part of a Globalized manoeuvre to align internal laws and external laws with international entities. In the UK the Health and Safety at Work etc. Act 1974 replaced The Factories etc. Act 1974 in 2011. In the USA the Occupational Safety and Health Act 1970 was amended through to 2004. The Canadian federal Occupational health and safety regulations have been constantly updated since 2019. Alberta and other States in Canada altered their existing occupational health and safety Acts between 2017-2023. For example, the Canadian Alberta state legislation, the Occupational Health and Safety Act 1976 underwent changes constantly until an attempt to modernise and harmonise began (Alberta Labour and Immigration, 2020). The harmonised laws in Australia were part of a bigger plan to bring similar laws not just within the Commonwealth but also within the geopolitical entity known as the Anglosphere.

In 2008 the Intergovernmental Agreement for Regulatory and Operational Reform in OHS was established. The Agreement involved: The Commonwealth Of Australia and the States Of New South Wales, Victoria, Queensland, Western Australia, South Australia, Tasmania, the Australian Capital Territory, and the Northern Territory Of Australia (Australia, 2008).

The key six objectives of the Agreement were to:

1. Improve OHS standards.
2. All parties are to have similar laws.
3. Laws will become harmonised.
4. Submissions to the Commonwealth Parliament to replace the Australian Safety and Compensation Council.
5. The parties mentioned agreed that workers' compensation would be dealt with separately.
6. Principles of cooperation and consultation between the parties to bring about the desired changes (Australia, 2008).

The fundamental objective of the agreement was to bring about reform to the current OHS Acts that existed in Australia. The criteria listed to determine this standard were

1. Enable the development of uniform, equitable, and effective safety standards.

2. Address compliance and regulatory burdens for employers with operations in more than one jurisdiction.
3. Create efficiencies for government to provide better OHS regulatory and support services.
4. Achieve continual reductions in the incidence of death, injury and disease through workplace activities (Australia, 2008).

In 18 May 2009, The Workplace Relations Minister Council agreed to a uniform OHS legislative framework (Australia, 2009). Between 2009 and 2012 there was the development of a Model Act and associated regulations. The Model law would be implemented in part or whole by the various jurisdictions in Australia. The Commonwealth of Australia, being the federal government of Australia adopted the Model Work Health and Safety Act in 2011.

Further Reading

Agricola, G. (1556). *De Re Metallica* (H. C. Hoover & L. H. Hoover, Trans.). The Mining Magazine.

Alberta Labour and Immigration. (2020). *Reforming the Occupational Health and Safety (OHS) Legislation in Alberta - Discussion Guide*. Alberta Labour and Immigration.

Australia. (2008). *Inter-Governmental Agreement for Regulatory and Operational Reform in Occupational Health and Safety* Federation of Australia. https://federation.gov.au/

Australia. (2009). *Occupational health and safety harmonisation*. Department of Employment and Workplace Relations,. https://www.dewr.gov.au/

Australian Bureau Of Statistics. (2023). *Work-related injuries*. Australian Bureau Of Statistics. https://www.abs.gov.au/

Bolt, J., & Zanden, J. L. v. (2024). *Gross domestic product (GDP) 1820 - 2022*. Our World In Data. https://ourworldindata.org/

Greasley, D., & Oxley, L. (1998). A tale of two dominions: comparing macroeconomic records of Australia and Canada since 1870. *Economic History Review*, 2, 294. https://people.stfx.ca/

Hammurabi. (1792 BC). *Code of Hammurabi* (R. F. Harper, Trans.). The University of Chicago Press.

Herodotus. (450BC). *Histories*. TUFTS University. https://www.perseus.tufts.edu/

Herodotus. (1920). *Histories* (A. D. Godley, Trans.). TUFTS University. https://www.perseus.tufts.edu/

Paracelsus. (1541). *Four treatises of Theophrastus von Hohenheim* (C. L. Temkin, G. Rosen, G. Zilboorg, & H. E. Sigerist, Trans.). Johns Hopkins Press. https://archive.org/

Ramazzini, B. (1700). *De Morbis Artificum Diatriba*. Typis A. Capponi. https://archive.org/

Robens, L. A. (1972). *Safety and health at work - report of the Committee, 1970-72*. In *Committee on Safety and Health at Work* H.M.S.O. https://archive.org/

Safe Work Australia. (2024b). *Key Work Health and Safety Statistics Australia 2024*. Safe Work Australia.

Australian States Legal Framework

The legal framework will be discussed along with the legislative system, the legislation, the judicial system and various important components of the framework. These important components will include the Duty of Care and Due and Diligence.

The Australian States legal framework places a basis or framework that all other components of Work Health and Safety will comply with. There are some universal truths such as breathing fresh air is good for us. Where this truth is compromised by dust or some contaminant in the air, the legal framework defines how to go about dealing with the issue. There, may be, multiple ways of doing something yet the ways revealed in this book are contemporary to the time it was written and the laws that applied at that time.

Legislative system

The legislative system is comprised of a parliament where all politicians sit. Parliament is divided into Government and Opposition. The government is the part of parliament in power. The opposition is comprised of those not directly in power but who have a seat in parliament. Usually, parliament is further divided into an upper and lower house where laws are made between the two houses. The upper house is often called the Senate and the Lower House is called the Legislative Assembly. This split of parliament is called a bicameral system. Not all states and territories use this system. The local councils are different in that the Assembly is formed by the public members and the council is formed by elected individuals (Parliamentary Education Office, 2024). More details will be provided.

Figure 4. *The tiers of parliament*

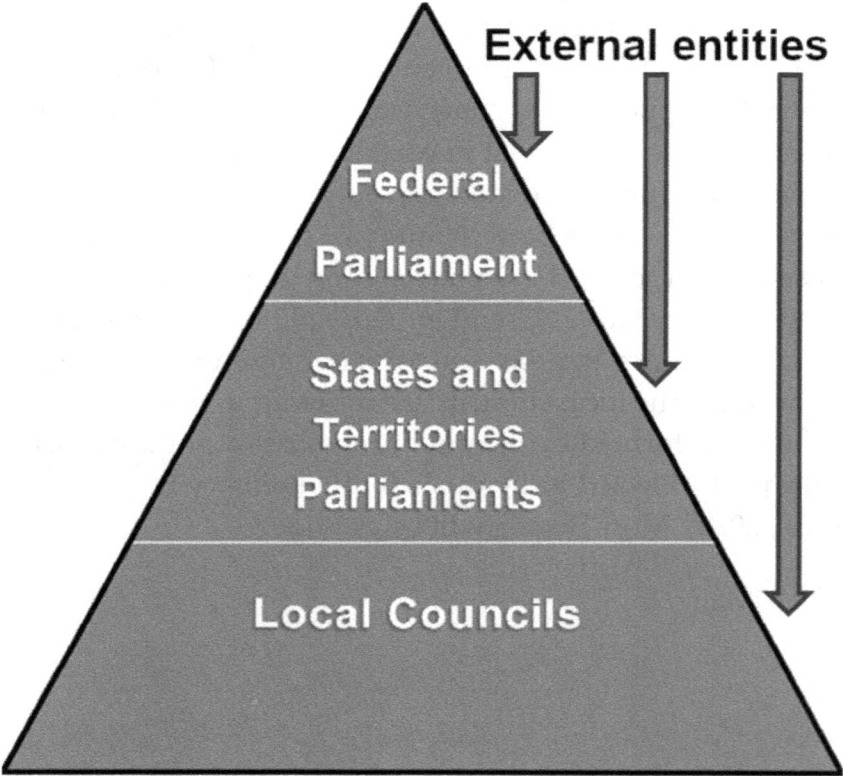

Federal Parliament

Federal parliament consists of the Commonwealth of Australia which hosts unelected external entities as the head of state and the Federation of Australia which is the Australian federated states and territories elected by the people. Often there is no distinction between the terms Commonwealth of Australia and the Federation of Australia.

Australia's government system has been described as many different things including a constitutional monarchy. At other times, it is considered a representative government system. In any case, the Oligarchical system has undergone significant changes since the colonisation of Australia began. The federation of the states and territories and the development of an elective process are potentially the two most significant changes to the system.

Figure 5. *Australian Senate*

(Harrison, 2012b)

Figure 6. *Australian House of Representatives*

(Harrison, 2012a)

State Parliament

All the states have a bicameral system except Queensland. The Australian Capital Territory and the Northern Territory do not have a bicameral system either. The unicameral states and territories use an elected Legislative Assembly sitting in one chamber.

The process for passing a law is slightly different per state. Not all unicameral processes are the same.

In Queensland, the system is as follows:

1. Presentation, explanatory speech and first reading:
2. Committee consideration:
3. Committee report:
4. Second reading:
5. consideration-in-detail:
6. third reading:
7. Royal Assent: (Queensland, 2024b).

In the Northern Territory, it is as follows:

1. **1st Reading**: The bill, which is an idea for a new law, is introduced into the Legislative Assembly.

2. **2nd Reading**: Members debate and vote on the main idea of the bill.

3. **Consideration in Detail**: Members examine the bill closely and may propose amendments.

4. **3rd Reading**: Members vote on the final version of the bill.

5. **Bill Passed**: If approved, the bill passes in the Legislative Assembly.

6. **Assent**: The Northern Territory Administrator signs the bill, making it a law for the Northern Territory (Northern Territory, 2024a).

In Bicameral systems such as those found in other states, they are similar to the Western Australian or Victorian Model.

The summarised Victorian model is:

1. 1st reading: Introduction of the bill
2. 2nd reading: Examining the principles
3. Consideration in detail
4. 3rd reading: Voting on the bill (Victoria, 2024a)

The Western Australian model is:

1. The Introduction and First Reading
2. The Second Reading
3. Committee of the Whole House
4. Referral to Other Committees
5. The Third Reading
6. Presentation to the Other House
7. Assent by the Governor
8. Proclamation (Western Australia, 2024b)

From this overview of the processes, we discover that the Territories ascent legislation or make it operative, through the Territory Administrator. Unlike the States where the Governor General is responsible for the ascent on behalf of the unelected Autocrat seated as the Head of the Commonwealth of Australia.

Local Council

Aside from the Australian Capital Territory (ACT), every other state and territory has a local government. The ACT has a division called City Services that takes care of local issues such as waste management. In all other States and territories, the local services are provided by a separate entity known as the Local Council or Shire Council. The Local council handles most domestic issues but must abide by the agenda and laws of the State.

Legislation

Figure 7. *The Hierarchy of Legislative Authority*

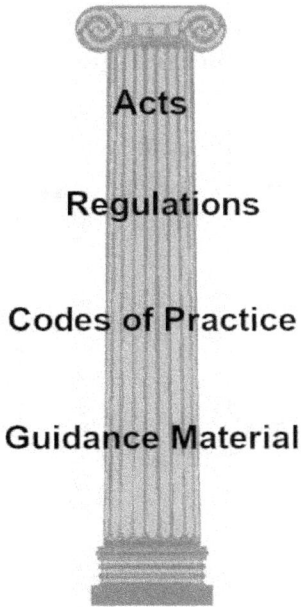

The Acts are the primary legislation, Regulations are secondary legislation, Codes of practice are tertiary legislation and Guidance materials and other standards can be subsidiary legislation.

If guidance materials and codes of practice are referenced by the regulations or Acts, then they are considered part of the law.

Common and Statute law

Statute law is the law that has been written down into Acts of Parliament. In other words, it is the law that usually comes from the Legislative Assembly. There are different ways of categorising the statutory laws. One way is to consider the Acts as primary law and all other referenced legislation as subsidiary. This is the most commonly accepted terminology. However, the terms Secondary and Tertiary are also used on occasions to describe the distance from the Primary law which is the Acts.

Common law also known as the "case law" or "law of the land" usually derives from the court system. It is a form of law that is based on court experience rather than the literal meanings of the statutes. The body of common law is made of several similar cases. Each case is unique; however, some commonalities are defined between cases and these common factors allow comparison of outcomes. In this way, a case is ruled one way based on specific criteria being met and ruled another way if another set of criteria are met. As the cases are judged, they form a precedence of similar cases. Precedence means that ruled based on how similar cases were ruled. In this way, the experience of the judges determines how a case is to be dealt with rather than basing it on the literal meaning of the statutes. In some cases, there are common law cases that do not exist in the statutes and as such claims or cases can be made based on common law alone.

Where Statutory law and common law cover the same aspects, Statutory law prevails. However, Statutory law has different ways of approaching it, such as through literal meanings, interpretive meanings and precedence. Although the statutes take priority, in many cases it can be argued through common law applications and through the way the law is approached by the judges.

Table 4

Differences between common and statute laws

WHS Common Law	WHS Statute Law
Reactive	Preventative
Negligence based	Compliance before Incident
Duty of Care Assumed to Exist	Meeting Duty of Care Explained

ACTS

The Acts are the laws passed by the government. These laws form the basis of the framework that the legal system will be developed upon. Acts are also known as Statutes. Statutes infer the written law.

Usually, the Acts are generic and will tackle problems in a general manner. When the statutes need to be specific and technical they usually rely on regulations to support the scope of application (*Work Health and Safety Act 2011*, Austl.).

As an example: *Work Health and Safety Act 2020* (Austl.) which is also cited as the *Work Health and Safety Act 2020* (Cth.) This book uses a reference to Australia as a federated entity by using the abbreviation Austl. Instead of a Commonwealth entity Cth.

Regulations

Regulations are secondary legislation and although not seen or handled as statutes, they form a binding relationship with the associated act that they support. For instance, the generic nature of the statute may be to require *"appropriate facilities"*, the regulations may specify that shade, access to water and temperature control measures are needed to provide *"appropriate facilities"* (*Work Health and Safety Regulations 2011*, Austl.).

As an example: The federal or commonwealth regulations for work health and safety; *Work Health and Safety Regulations 2011* (Austl).

Codes of Practice

Codes of practice are usually a more in-depth risk treatment for a particular topic such as confined space management or excavation work etc. An example of an approved Code of Practice is the *Work Health and Safety (Confined Spaces) Code of Practice 2015 (Work Health and Safety Act 2011, Austl., s.274).*

Other subjects covered by the approved Federal Codes of Practice up to the time of writing include:

1. How to Manage Work Health and Safety Risks Code of Practice 2015
2. Work Health and Safety Consultation, Co-operation and Co-ordination Code of Practice 2015
3. Abrasive Blasting Code of Practice 2015
4. Confined Spaces Code of Practice 2015
5. Construction Work Code of Practice 2015
6. Demolition Work Code of Practice 2015
7. Excavation Work Code of Practice 2015

8. First Aid in the Workplace Code of Practice 2015
9. Hazardous Manual Tasks Code of Practice 2015
10. How to Manage and Control Asbestos in the Workplace Code of Practice 2015
11. How to Safely Remove Asbestos Code of Practice 2015
12. Labelling of Workplace Hazardous Chemicals Code of Practice 2015
13. Managing Electrical Risks in the Workplace Code of Practice 2015
14. Managing Noise and Preventing Hearing Loss at Work Code of Practice 2015
15. Managing Risks in Stevedoring Code of Practice 2017
16. Managing Risks of Hazardous Chemicals in the Workplace Code of Practice 2015
17. Managing Risks of Plant in the Workplace Code of Practice 2015
18. Managing the Risk of Falls at Workplaces Code of Practice 2015
19. Managing the Work Environment and Facilities Code of Practice 2015
20. Preparation of Safety Data Sheets for Hazardous Chemicals Code of Practice 2015
21. Preventing Falls in Housing Construction Code of Practice 2015
22. Safe Design of Structures Code of Practice 2015
23. Spray Painting and Powder Coating Code of Practice 2015
24. Welding Processes Code of Practice 2015,

Guidance Material

Guidance material is usually not law on its own unless it is referenced by the Statute or regulations. If that is the case then the guidance material such as those found in the Australian Standards publications are considered a part of the law.

As an example the Australian and New Zealand Standards referenced in the national regulations are; AS/NZS 1200:2015 Pressure equipment   (*Work Health and Safety Regulations 2011*, Austl., sch. 5 pt. 2).

Table 5

Referenced Standards in the Model WHS Regulations

Australian / Joint New Zealand Standard	Title	WHS Regulation
AS 1200:2015	*Pressure equipment*	Schedule 5 Part 2
AS/NZS 1269.1:2005	*Occupational noise management – Measurement and assessment of noise emission and exposure*	Regulation 56
AS/NZS 1716:2012	*Respiratory protective devices*	Regulation 184A
AS/NZS 1891.1:2020	*Personal equipment for work at height – Manufacturing requirements for full body combination and lower body harnesses*	Regulation 221
AS 2030.1:2009	*Gas cylinders – General requirements*	Regulation 5 Schedule 5 Part 1
AS/NZS 2299.1:2015	*Occupational diving operations – Standard operational practice*	Regulation 5
AS 2397:2015	*Safe use of lasers in the building and construction industry*	Regulation 223
AS 2593:2021	*Boilers – Safety management and supervision systems*	Regulation 5 Regulation 15 (note)

AS 2700S–2011	Colour standards for general purposes (R13) and (Y11)	Schedule 13 Part 3 Schedule 13 Part 5
AS/NZS 2815	Training and certification of occupational divers	Regulation 171
AS 2832.1:2015	Cathodic protection of metals – Pipes and cables	Regulation 144
AS/NZS 3012:2019	Electrical installations – Construction and demolition sites	Regulation 163
AS 3533.1:2009	Amusement rides and devices – Design and construction	Schedule 5 Part 1 Schedule 5 Part 2
AS/NZS 2815	Training and certification of recreational divers	Regulation 171
AS 4343:2014	Pressure equipment – Hazard levels	Schedule 5 Part 1 Schedule 5 Part 2
AS 4801:2001	Occupational health and safety management systems	Regulation 5
AS 4964:2004	Method for the qualitative identification of asbestos in bulk samples	Regulation 419

(Safe Work Australia, 2023a).

Jurisdictions and Regulators

There are nine broad legal jurisdictions for WHS.
Commonwealth, ACT, NSW, NT, Qld, SA, TAS, Vic and
WA. The Commonwealth *Work Health and Safety Act 2011
(Austl.)* and the *Work Health and Safety Regulations 2011
(Austl.)* apply only to commonwealth or federal businesses
or undertakings. This means that if an entity such as a
worker or PCBU does work for the Commonwealth or
Federal Government, they will be covered by the application
of these Acts and Regulations. The relationship can be direct
or indirect so that if a private company is working for the
Commonwealth or a shared project between the
Commonwealth and State, then the application of these
Commonwealth laws takes precedence (*Work Health and
Safety Act 2011*, Austl.).

The State laws apply in all other situations in every
workplace within the state. Aside from shared ventures,
with the Commonwealth, the State laws will apply. In some
cases, the Commonwealth laws empower the States to bind
the Crown to their State laws such as the Road Transport
Reform (Dangerous Goods) Act 1995 No. 34, 1995 - Sect 7
(*Road Transport Reform (Dangerous Goods) ACT 1995 No. 34*,
2024). The Northern Territory and Australian Capital
Territory are exceptions to this general rule because they
only use their territorial laws and not the Commonwealth
laws (*Work Health and Safety Act 2011*, Austl., s.12).

"7.(1) This Act binds the Crown in all its capacities.

(2) It is intended that an adopting law of a State or of the Northern Territory will bind the Crown in all its capacities.

(3) For that purpose, an adopting law of a State or of the Northern Territory may bind the Crown in right of the Commonwealth."(*Road Transport Reform (Dangerous Goods) ACT 1995 No. 34*, 2024).

The following tables attempt to capture the most commonly used state laws. Each State has a set of Acts, regulations, codes of practice and guidance material. However, the scope of this book is to introduce the state legislation and not to thoroughly cover each and every topic under the WHS legislation. A set of over twenty Codes of Practice have been omitted for each state, however, to get an idea of their content the model Codes of Practice have been listed. Note also that the model Codes of Practice are not the same for each State's equivalent Code of Practice.

Furthermore, a common theme with the legislation at the time of writing was to have tied the mining and general WHS laws together in some manner. Some continue to have separate laws others have incorporated them together. Queensland, New South Wales and Western Australia have separate State mining legislation. Further in the list of tables is also a commonwealth section which has a significant number of relevant Mining-related Acts that apply to all States. In 2013 the ACT, Commonwealth, NSW, and NT attempted to harmonize their mining legislation. This in some cases meant the development of a single act for WHS but different mining-related regulations. In other instances, the mining and general WHS Acts were combined such as in Victoria.

Generally, the Australian Government is responsible for offshore mineral and petroleum exploration and mining. Onshore mining legislation is managed by the individual states and territories.

Concerning the topic of Dangerous Goods and Transport, Storage and Handling, there is a federal law that empowers state laws on the matter.

Australian Capital Territory (ACT)

Table 6

Regulator 2024: WorkSafe (ACT) - Legislation

Act	Secondary
Work Health and Safety Act 2011 (ACT)	*Work Health and Safety Regulation 2011 (ACT)*
Scaffolding and Lifts Act 1912	*Scaffolding and Lifts Regulation 1950*
Machinery Act 1949	*Machinery Regulation 1950* *Boilers and Pressure Vessels Regulation 1954*
Dangerous Goods (Road Transport Act) 2009	*Dangerous Goods (Road Transport) Regulation 2010*
Dangerous Substances Act 2004	

(Worksafe (ACT), 2024).

New South Wales (NSW)

Table 7

Regulator 2024: SafeWork (NSW) - Legislation

Act	Secondary
Work Health and Safety Act 2011 (NSW)	*Work Health and Safety Regulation 2017 (NSW)*
Work Health and Safety (Mines and Petroleum Sites) Act 2013	*Work Health and Safety (Mines and Petroleum Sites) Regulation 2022*
Explosives Act 2003	*Explosives Regulation 2013.*
Rural Workers Accommodation Act 1969	
Dangerous Goods (Road and Rail Transport) Act 2008	*Dangerous Goods (Road and Rail Transport) Regulation 2014.*
Mining Act 1992	
Coal Mine Health and Safety Act 2002 No 129	
Petroleum (Onshore) Act 1991	
Radiation Control Act 1990	
Explosives Act 2003	*Explosives Regulation 2013*

(SafeWork (NSW), 2024).

Northern Territory (NT)

Table 8

Regulator 2024: WorkSafe (NT) - Legislation

Act	Secondary
Work Health and Safety (National Uniform Legislation) Act 2011 (NT)	*Work Health and Safety (National Uniform Legislation) Regulations 2011 (NT)* *Code of Practice: Managing psychosocial hazards at work*
Electricity Reform Act 2000	*Electricity Reform (Safety and Technical) Regulations 2000*
Dangerous Goods Act 1998	*Dangerous Goods Regulations 1985*
Transport of Dangerous Goods by Road and Rail (National Uniform Legislation) Act 2010	*Transport of Dangerous Goods by Road and Rail (National Uniform Legislation) Regulations 2011*

(Worksafe (NT), 2024).

Queensland (Qld)

Table 9

Regulator 2024: WorkSafe (Qld.) - Legislation

Act	Secondary
Work Health and Safety Act 2011	Work Health and Safety Regulation 2011
Coal Mining Safety and Health Act 1999	Coal Mining Safety and Health Regulation 2017
Mining and Quarrying Safety and Health Act 1999	Mining and Quarrying Safety and Health Regulation 2017
Explosives Act 1999	
Radiation Safety Act 1999	
Work Health and Safety and Other Legislation Amendment Act 2024	
Transport Operations (Road Use Management) Act 1995	Transport Operations (Road Use Management – Dangerous Goods) Regulation 2018
Transport Infrastructure Act 1994	Transport Infrastructure (Dangerous Goods by Rail) Regulation 2018

(Queensland, 2024c; Worksafe (Qld), 2024).

In addition to the generic Model Codes of Practice Queensland has modified new versions for those tabled here:

Table 10

Referenced Modified Codes of Practice in Queensland

Codes of Practice (2023-2024)
Construction and operation of Solar Farms Code of Practice 2024
Amusement devices code of practice 2023
Managing respirable dust hazards in coal-fired power stations Code of Practice 2023
Concrete pumping code of practice 2019
Managing the risk of psychosocial hazards at work code of practice 2022
Managing respirable crystalline silica dust exposure in construction and manufacturing of construction elements Code of Practice 2022

(Worksafe (Qld), 2024).

South Australia (SA)

Table 11

Regulator 2024: SafeWork (SA) - Legislation

Act	Secondary
Work Health and Safety Act 2012	*Work Health and Safety Regulations 2012*
Mines and Works Inspection Act 1920	*Mines and Works Inspection Regulations 2013*
Dangerous Substances Act 1979	*Dangerous Substances (General) Regulations 2017* *Dangerous Substances (Fees) Regulations 2017* *Dangerous Substances (Dangerous Goods Transport) Regulations 2023*
Explosives Act 1936	*Explosives (Security Sensitive Substances) Regulations 2021* *Explosives Regulations 2011* *Explosives (Fireworks) Regulations 2016*
Petroleum Products Regulation Act 1995	*Petroleum Products Regulations 2023*
Employment Agents Registration Act 1993	*Employment Agents Registration Regulations 2010*

(SafeWork (SA), 2024).

Tasmania (TAS)

Table 12

Regulator 2024: WorkSafe (Tas.) - Legislation

Act	Secondary
Work Health and Safety Act 2012	*Work Health and Safety Regulations 2022*
Work Health and Safety (Transitional and Consequential Provisions) Act 2012	*Work Health and Safety (Transitional) Regulations 2022*
Dangerous Goods (Road and Rail Transport) Act 2010	*Dangerous Goods (Road and Rail Transport) Regulations 2021*
Explosives Act 2012	*Explosives Regulations 2022*
Mines Work Health and Safety (Supplementary Requirements) Act 2012	*Mines Work Health and Safety (Supplementary Requirements) Regulations 2022*
Security-sensitive Dangerous Substances Act 2005	*Security-sensitive Dangerous Substances Regulations 2015*

(Worksafe (TAS), 2024).

Victoria (VIC)

Table 13

Regulator 2024: WorkSafe (Vic.) – Legislation

Act	Secondary
Occupational Health and Safety Act 2004	*Occupational Health and Safety Regulations 2017* *Chapter 5.3 (Mines) of the Occupational Health and Safety Regulations 2017*
Equipment (Public Safety) Act 1994	*Equipment (Public Safety) Regulations 2017*
Dangerous Goods Act 1985	*Dangerous Goods (HCDG) Regulations 2016* *Dangerous Goods (Explosives) Regulations 2022* *Dangerous Goods (Transport by Road or Rail) Regulations 2018* *Dangerous Goods (Storage and Handling) Regulations 2022*
	Magistrates' Court (Occupational Health and Safety) Rules 2015

(Worksafe (VIC), 2024).

Western Australia (WA)

Table 14

Regulator 2024: WorkSafe (WA) - Legislation

Act	Secondary
Work Health and Safety Act 2020	Work Health and Safety (General) Regulations 2022 Work Health and Safety (Mines) Regulations 2022 and Work Health and Safety (Petroleum and Geothermal Energy Operations) Regulations 2022
Dangerous Goods Safety Act 2004	Dangerous Goods Safety (Storage and Handling of Non-explosives) Regulations 2007 Dangerous Goods Safety (Road and Rail Transport of Non-Explosives) Regulations 2007 Dangerous Goods Safety (Major Hazard Facilities) Regulations 2007 Dangerous Goods Safety (Explosives) Regulations 2007 Dangerous Goods Safety (Security Sensitive Ammonium Nitrate) Regulations 2007 Dangerous Goods Safety (General) Regulations 2007

Please note that each state and territory have different approved Codes of Practice. These model codes of practice are only listed to guide as to the minimum areas that most State COPs cover.

Table 15

Model Codes of Practice

Model Codes of Practice
Abrasive blasting
Confined spaces
Construction work
Demolition work
Excavation work
First aid in the workplace
Hazardous manual tasks
How to manage and control asbestos in the workplace
How to manage work health and safety risks
How to safely remove asbestos
Labelling of workplace hazardous chemicals
Managing electrical risks in the workplace
Managing noise and preventing hearing loss at work
Managing psychosocial hazards at work
Managing risks in stevedoring
Managing risks of hazardous chemicals in the workplace

Managing risks of plant in the workplace

Managing the risk of falls at workplaces

Managing the risk of falls in housing construction

Managing the risks of respirable crystalline silica from engineered stone in the workplace

Managing the work environment and facilities

Preparation of safety data sheets for hazardous chemicals

Safe design of structures

Sexual and gender-based harassment

Spray painting and powder coating

Tower cranes

Welding processes

Work health and safety consultation, cooperation and coordination

(Safe Work Australia, 2024a)

Commonwealth / Australian Laws

Table 16

Regulator 2024: ComCare (Cth.) - Legislation

Act	Secondary
Work Health and Safety Act 2011 (Cth./Austl.)	*Work Health and Safety Regulations 2011 (Cth./Austl.)*
Mining Act 1978	*Mining Regulations 1981*
Offshore Minerals Act 2003	
Offshore Petroleum and Greenhouse Gas Storage Act 2006	*Work Health and Safety (Petroleum and Geothermal Energy Operations) Regulations 2022*
Road Transport Reform (Dangerous Goods) Act 1995	*Australian Code for the Transport of Dangerous Goods by Road & Rail 7.8*

Note: State Laws with similar names exist for the Commonwealth or National legislation listed here. They are different and have different jurisdictions.

Judicial system

The judicial system will listen to civil and criminal matters. Civil matters usually do not involve the government as one of the parties. Civil matters may include a variety of cases. The cases maybe a part of laws other than those directly related to work health and safety. The general areas of Law are;

Torts and Negligence Law

Compensation claims against another party are usually based on negligence.

Contract Law

Dispute resolution over contracts. It may involve injury or damages compensation.

Land and Property Law

Dealings with property and possible compensation.

Family Law

Concerning family matters that may involve compensation.

Constitutional Law

Most Civil cases have some common elements to them, that include;

Criminal law as it applies to WHS almost always involves the government. The process is to determine if a situation or incident was considered criminal and this may include breaches of the statutory law as well as some cases using common law.

The brief comparison between Civil and Criminal cases is tabled below.

Table 17

Comparison between Civil and Criminal cases

Property	Civil	Criminal
Definition	Involves a dispute such as a Party A v Party B	Prosecution such as State v Defendant
Purpose	Compensation and Deterrent	Punishment and Deterrent
Standard of Proof	Beyond balance of probability	Beyond reasonable doubt
Burden of Proof	Claimant provides evidence	Defendant is innocent until proven guilty
Outcome	Compensation	Punishment such as fines, imprisonment and community service

There are three courts in most states. A higher state court is called a Supreme Court, an intermediate court is usually called a District Court and a Magistrates or Local Court. The Australian Capital Territory, Tasmania and Northern Territory do not have an intermediate court.

Local Court

Local Court usually tied to the operations of small claims and local government laws, known as bylaws. The local courts are an extension of the Magistrates courts and normally deal with minor incidents and claims. The cap amount claimable within the local courts varies.

Magistrates Court

The magistrates' court and its jurisdiction vary across Australia. Usually when matters are more serious and involve claims over a capped amount between $10,000 and $25,000 across Australia, then the magistrates court hears such matters. Otherwise, they may be heard in Local courtrooms.

District Court

The intermediate court is present in most but not all states. Tasmania, NT, and ACT, as already stated, don't have a district court system. In all other places, the District Court hears moderate to serious cases, usually but not always involving matters with high monetary claims or serious incidents.

Supreme Court

The highest-level court within the state system or territory system is the Supreme Court. In places that don't have a District court the Supreme Court hears more cases of moderate to serious matters along with appeals. The Supreme Court in places with a District Court tend to hear cases of serious and costly matters. The Supreme Courts also listen to appeals and, in some instances, there are separate Supreme Appeal courts as found in the ACT. There is an overlap between the Supreme Courts and the High Courts in that the cases brought before the Supreme Court may involve Federal matters but not always. For example, a terrorism Case S37/2024 HC Australia sentenced a person from within the Supreme courts of New South Wales that eventually reached the High court of Australia.

High Court

The high courts of Australia are the federal courts and usually involve three branches: Federal Court, Family court and the Court of Appeal. Federal courts hear matters associated with work, employment and federal legislation. Family courts deal with family legislation and issues. The Court of Appeal involves a broad spectrum of cases civil and criminal that impact more than the case itself but other Australians.

State courts

Australian Capital Territory (ACT)

Table 18

ACT State courts

Court	Description
Supreme Court	Supreme Court
	Court of Appeal
Magistrates Court	Magistrates Court
	Coroners Court
	Children's Court
	Industrial Court
	Galambany Court
	Family Violence Court

(Australian Capital Territory, 2024).

New South Wales (NSW)

Table 19

NSW State courts

Court	Description
Supreme Court	Supreme Court Court of Appeal
District Court	Civil and Criminal Cases
Local Court	Civil and Criminal Cases
Tribunals and Other	Land and Environment Court Industrial Relations Commission Coroner's Court Dust Diseases Tribunal

(New South Wales, 2024)

Northern Territory (NT)

Table 20

NT State courts

Court	Description
Supreme Court	Supreme Court Court of Appeal
Local Court	Civil and Criminal Cases
Other	Work Health Court Youth Justice Court

(Northern Territory, 2024b)

Queensland (Qld.)

Table 21

Qld. State courts

Court	Description
Supreme Court	Supreme Court
	Court of Appeal
District Court	Civil and Criminal Cases
Magistrate	Civil and Criminal Cases
Tribunals and Other	Industrial Court
	Industrial Relations Commission
	Planning and Environment Court
	Land Appeal Court
	Land Court
	Drug and Alcohol Court
	Coroners Court
	Children's Court
	Mental Health Court
	Murri Court
	Specialist Domestic and Family Violence Specialist Court
	Queensland Civil Administration Tribunal

(Queensland, 2024a)

South Australia (SA)

Table 22

SA State courts

Court	Description
Supreme Court	Supreme Court Court of Appeal
District Court	Civil and Criminal Cases
Magistrate	Civil and Criminal Cases
Other	Environment, Resources and Development (ERD) Youth Court Coroners Court Wardens Court

(Courts Administration Authority of South Australia, 2024)

Tasmania (TAS)

Table 23

TAS State courts

Court	Description
Supreme Court	Supreme Court
	Court of Appeal
Magistrates Court	Civil and Criminal Cases
Tribunals and Other	Anti-Discrimination Tribunal
	Asbestos Compensation Tribunal
	Forestry Practices Tribunal
	Guardianship & Administration Board
	Health Practitioners Tribunal
	Mental Health Tribunal
	Motor Accidents Compensation Tribunal
	Resource Management and Planning Appeal Tribunal
	Workers Rehabilitation and Compensation Tribunal

(Tasmania, 2024)

Victoria (VIC)

Table 24

VIC State courts

Court	Description
Supreme Court	Supreme Court Court of Appeal
County Court	Civil and Criminal Cases
Magistrates Court	Civil and Criminal Cases
Other	Children's Court Coroners Court Victorian Civil and Administrative Tribunal Victims of Crime Assistance Tribunal

(Victoria, 2024b)

Western Australia (WA)

Table 25

WA State courts

Court	Description
Supreme Court	Supreme Court Court of Appeal
District Court	Civil and Criminal Cases
Magistrates Court	Civil and Criminal Cases
Other	Warden's Court Coroner's Court Children's Court

(Western Australia, 2024a)

Further Reading

Australian Capital Territory. (2024). *ACT Courts.* https://www.courts.act.gov.au/

Courts Administration Authority of South Australia. (2024). *Our Courts.* South Australia. https://www.courts.sa.gov.au/our-courts/

Harrison, J. (2012a). Australian House of Representatives.

Harrison, J. (2012b). Australian Senate.

New South Wales. (2024). *Communities and Justice.* https://courts.nsw.gov.au/

Northern Territory. (2024a). *Making a law in the Northern Territory.* Parliamentary Education Services. https://parliament.nt.gov.au/

Northern Territory. (2024b). *Types of courts and their roles.* https://nt.gov.au/law/courts-and-tribunals/types-of-courts-and-their-roles

Parliamentary Education Office. (2024). *The responsibilities of the three levels of government.* Federation of Australia. https://peo.gov.au/

Queensland. (2024a). *Courts.* Queensland. https://www.courts.qld.gov.au/courts

Queensland. (2024b). *The Legislative Process - The Making of a Law (simplified).* Queensland Parliament. https://documents.parliament.qld.gov.au/

Queensland. (2024c). *Road and rail laws for dangerous goods.* Queensland. https://www.business.qld.gov.au

Road Transport Reform (Dangerous Goods) ACT 1995 No. 34. (2024). Retrieved from http://www.austlii.edu.au/

Safe Work Australia. (2023a). *Australia and other standards.* Safe Work Australia.

Safe Work Australia. (2024a). *Codes of Practice.* Safe Work Australia,. https://www.safeworkaustralia.gov.au/law-and-regulation/codes-practice

SafeWork (NSW). (2024). *Legislation.* New South Wales. https://www.safework.nsw.gov.au/

SafeWork (SA). (2024). *Legislation.* https://www.safework.sa.gov.au/

Tasmania, J. D. o. (2024). *Courts and Tribunals Tasmania.* https://www.courts.tas.gov.au/

Victoria. (2024a). *How a law is made.* Parliament of Victoria. https://www.parliament.vic.gov.au/

Victoria. (2024b). *Victorian courts and tribunals.* Victoria. https://courts.vic.gov.au/court-system/victorian-courts-and-tribunals

Western Australia. (2024a). *Court System in Western Australia.* Western Australia,. https://www.supremecourt.wa.gov.au/

Western Australia. (2024b). *The Legislative Process.* Parliament of Western Australia. https://www.parliament.wa.gov.au/

Work Health and Safety Act 2011. (Austl.).

Work Health and Safety Regulations 2011. (Austl.).

Worksafe (ACT). (2024). *Legislation.* Australian Capital Territory. https://www.worksafe.act.gov.au/

Worksafe (NT). (2024). *Laws and compliance.* Northern Territory. https://worksafe.nt.gov.au/

Worksafe (Qld). (2024). *Work Health and Safety Laws.* Queensland. https://www.worksafe.qld.gov.au/

Worksafe (TAS). (2024). *Acts and Regulations.* Tasmania. https://worksafe.tas.gov.au/

Worksafe (VIC). (2024). *All Acts and Regulations.* Victoria. https://www.worksafe.vic.gov.au/

Common Legal terms

There are many legal terms involved with Work Health and Safety. Rather than create a list of definitions, or attempt to be a definitive reference, the scope is to provide a generic background of the law. Furthermore, a careful selection of terms is discussed. The selection criteria for the terms have been based on their appearance in legislation and common law and their relevance to the WHS professional. Being legal terms they have a substantial amount of information that defines them. Large volumes of information may exist for specific terms and as such specialised knowledge is needed to interpret them. It is beyond the purpose of this book to deliver the exact way that these terms are used in courts. Instead, we are merely investigating and discussing the known terms as they apply to work health and safety laws and to the work health and safety professional.

Duty of Care

A duty of care has developed through laws stemming from the United Kingdom. A duty of care is an onus to another person or party that has a proximity or neighbourly relation to the person. In some cases, the duty to care is reciprocated or owed by both parties in a relationship. It can be owed by more than one party and it can be owed to more than one party. It is a non-delegable duty.

Important common law cases that established the Duty of Care include;

Smith v Charles Baker & Sons (1891): Emphasized the importance of warning employees about dangers associated with their work (*Smith v Charles Baker & Sons*, 1891) .

Donoghue v Stevenson (1932): Established the general principles of negligence, including the duty of care owed to one's neighbour (*Donoghue v Stevenson*, 1932).

Grant v Australian Knitting Mills (1936): Applied the principles of negligence to manufacturers, which has implications for workplace safety regarding equipment and materials and resources (*Grant v Australian Knitting Mills*, 1936) .

Wilsons & Clyde Coal Co v English (1938): Defined an employer's duty of care to provide a safe system of work, competent staff, and adequate materials (*Wilsons & Clyde Coal Co v English*, 1938).

Paris v Stepney Borough Council (1951): Highlighted the employer's duty to consider the individual circumstances of employees when assessing risks and the suitable provision of personal protective equipment (*Paris v Stepney BC*, 1951).

Bolton v Stone (1951): Addressed the likelihood of harm and reasonable precautions to those of proximity in duty of care (*Stone v Bolton*, 1951).

Latimer v AEC Ltd (1953): It was an unsuccessful appeal, that establishes what is considered reasonable. The case dealt with the reasonableness of precautions taken by an employer to prevent accidents (*Latimer v AEC Ltd*, 1953).

Watt v Hertfordshire County Council (1954): Considered the balance between risk and the necessity of an act. The acceptance of certain risks was established (*Watt v Hertfordshire County Council*, 1954).

Hamilton v Nuroof (WA) Pty Ltd (1956): An Australian case that clarified the employer's duty to take reasonable care to avoid exposing employees to unreasonable risks of injury (*Hamilton v Nuroof (WA) Pty Ltd*, 1956).

Atlas Roofing Co. v. Occupational Safety and Health Review Comm'n (1977): Although a USA case and of less impact to the Australian states, it establishes the purposes of a Regulator and public rights. Generally, it discussed the authority of an executive agency over adjudicating violations of public rights statutes.

Caparo Industries plc v Dickman (1990): Refined the test for duty of care, focusing on foreseeability, proximity, and whether it is fair, just, and reasonable to impose a duty (*Caparo Industries plc v Dickman*, 1990).

Connelly v RTZ Corporation plc (1997): Recognized the duty of care owed by parent companies for the health and safety of employees of their subsidiaries (*Connelly v RTZ Corporation Plc and Others*, 1997).

In Australia, all the states and territories are influenced by the historical precedence of these common law cases. In addition, changes to the statutes to reflect these and many other cases have led to a uniform acceptance of a duty of care, especially for an employer or person conducting a business or undertaking.

Using the harmonised model laws the duty of care is defined as: ensuring so far as is practicable the health and safety of workers and those affected by the work being done by the PCBU. Also, that health and safety of the workers and other persons is not put at risk by the work done. This includes:

1.   Providing and maintaining a healthy and safe work environment

2.   Providing and maintaining safe plant and structures

3.   Provision and maintenance of safe systems of work

4.   Ensuring the safe use, handling and storage of plant, structures and substances

5.   Provision of adequate facilities for the welfare of workers

6.   Providing Information, training, instruction or supervision to perform work

7.   Monitoring to ensure workplace conditions (*Model Work Health and Safety Act 2011*, Austl.).

Person Conducting a Business or Undertaking (PCBU)

From the time of the harmonised legislation, differing by state, the use of the term Person Conducting a Business or Undertaking (PCBU) has been used. It replaces and enhances the concept of the employer and employee relationship. Based on the changes through common law, the concept of negligence and duty of care has been transformed. The duty of care was owed by anyone conducting a business or undertaking to both those working and those in legal proximity to that business or undertaking. The term employer was replaced by Person Conducting a Business or Undertaking (PCBU). This term is used for both profit a non-profit operations or businesses.

According to the Model Act 2022 Bill, the definition is set out as follows:

"(1) … a person conducts a business or undertaking:

> (a) whether the person conducts the business or undertaking alone or with others; and

> (b) whether or not the business or undertaking is conducted for profit or gain.

(2) A business or undertaking conducted by a person includes a business or undertaking conducted by a partnership or an unincorporated association.

(3) If a business or undertaking is conducted by a partnership (other than an incorporated partnership), a reference in this Act to a person conducting the business or undertaking is to be read as a reference to each partner in the partnership.

(4) A person does not conduct a business or undertaking to the extent that the person is engaged solely as a worker in, or as an officer of, that business or undertaking."

(5) An elected member of a local authority does not in that capacity conduct a business or undertaking.

(6) The regulations may specify the circumstances in which a person may be taken not to be a person who conducts a business or undertaking for the purposes of this Act or any provision of this Act.

(7) A volunteer association does not conduct a business or undertaking for the purposes of this Act.

(8) In this section, volunteer association means a group of volunteers working together for 1 or more community purposes where none of the volunteers, whether alone or jointly with any other volunteers, employs any person to carry out work for the volunteer association" (*Model Work Health and Safety Bill 2022*, Austl.).

The above means that all partners in a partnership are considered PCBU unless in an incorporated partnership. Officers and workers are not considered PCBUs. Purely volunteer associations are not considered PCBUs. Incorporated Associations are not considered a PCBU. Even if WHS does not apply to a workplace by WHS statutes, does not necessarily mean it is not covered by common law or other statutes.

Also, it should be noted that Victorian laws do not use the term PCBU. Instead, other terms are used as they suit the scenario or topic. The most common replacement term is Employer to mean something similar to PCBU but as described elsewhere they are different. Other terms include provider and workplace. The Victorian laws also define operations in other associated legislation by tiers and each one has specific expectations (*Labour Hire Licensing Act 2018*, Vic.).

Worker and Employee

From time-to-time worker and employee are used interchangeably, however, since harmonisation, they are two different entities. An employee is someone directly employed by an employer. A worker can mean anyone who is employed or otherwise working for either an employer or on a business or undertaking. Both employee and worker can be used for paid and unpaid positions. The term employee is usually used when strict contracts, roles and responsibilities apply to the position. Worker is a more flexible term in that it can be anyone engaged officially by written contract or otherwise.

The Victorian legislation does not use the harmonised term PCBU also it avoids using the term employee. Often the WHS laws in Victoria use the term worker to mean more or less the same as worker in harmonised laws.

"… (1) An individual is a worker, for a provider, if

(a) an arrangement is in force between the individual and the provider under which the provider supplies, or may supply, the individual to one or more other persons to perform work; and

(b) the provider is obliged to pay the individual (in whole or part) for the performance of the work by the individual, whether directly or indirectly through one or more intermediaries.

(2) An individual is a worker, for a provider, if an arrangement is in force between the individual and the provider under which the provider —

(a) recruits the individual for, or places the individual with, one or more other persons to perform work, being persons who are obliged to pay the individual (in whole or part) for the performance of the work by the individual, whether directly or indirectly through one or more intermediaries; or

(b) recruits the individual as an independent contractor for one or more other persons to perform work, and manages the contract performance by the independent contractor.

(3) For the purposes of this section, an individual may be a worker for a provider regardless of the following —

(a) whether the individual is an employee of the provider;

(b) whether a contract has been entered into between the individual and the provider;

(c) whether the individual is an apprentice, or is under a training contract, within the meaning of the Education and Training Reform Act 2006 (*Labour Hire Licensing Act 2018*, Vic., s.9)."

Note that the definition of worker in the *Occupational Health and Safety Act 2004* (Vic.) refers to the definition found in the *Labour Hire Licensing Act 2018* (Vic.). It also references the *Education and Reform Act 2006* (Vic.) for the definition of a training contract" (*Occupational Health and Safety Act 2004*, Vic., s.5).

The worker in harmonised legislation is defined as;

"(1) A person is a *worker* if the person carries out work in any capacity for a person conducting a business or undertaking, including work as:

(a) an employee; or

(b) a contractor or subcontractor; or

(c) an employee of a contractor or subcontractor; or

(d) an employee of a labour hire company who has been assigned to work in the person's business or undertaking; or

(e) an outworker; or

(f) an apprentice or trainee; or

(g) a student gaining work experience; or

(h) a volunteer; or

(i) a person of a prescribed class.

(2) For the purposes of this Act, a police officer is:

(a) a worker; and

(b) at work throughout the time when the officer is on duty or lawfully performing the functions of a police officer, but not otherwise.

(3) The person conducting the business or undertaking is also a *worker* if the person is an individual who carries out work in that business or undertaking" (*Model Work Health and Safety Bill 2022*, Austl., s.7).

For most cases and in most circumstances, we can presume that the term *worker* has the same broad meaning throughout Australia. Some differences should be noted such as that used in Victoria because legally different approaches and words imply different laws and interpretations by judges. When there is doubt over a definition the regulator for each state or territory is an important consultative partner.

Officer

Corporations

An officer in most legislation is determined by the same definition given in the Corporations Act 2001 (Austl.). The term corporate collective investment vehicle (CCIV) used as part of defining an officer is a type of registration that a corporation can be registered as.

"(1) An officer of a corporation (other than a CCIV) is:

(a) a director or secretary of the corporation; or

(b) a person:

(i) who makes, or participates in making, decisions that affect the whole, or a substantial part, of the business of the corporation; or

(ii) who has the capacity to affect significantly the corporation's financial standing; or

(iii) in accordance with whose instructions or wishes the directors of the corporation are accustomed to act (excluding advice given by the person in the proper performance of functions attaching to the person's professional capacity or their business relationship with the directors or the corporation);..." (*Corporations Act 2001*, Austl., s.9AD).

Commonwealth

Concerning the term *officer* in a Commonwealth context;

"(1) A person who makes, or participates in making, decisions that affect the whole, or a substantial part, of a business or undertaking of the Commonwealth is taken to be an officer of the Commonwealth for the purposes of this Act.

(2) Subject to subsection (3), a Minister of a State or the Commonwealth is not in that capacity an officer for the purposes of this Act.

(3) To avoid doubt, a parliamentarian is an officer of the Commonwealth for the purposes of this Act in respect of the business or undertaking of the Commonwealth constituted by the provision by the Commonwealth of support for the functioning of the Parliament.

(4) Subsection (3) does not limit:

(a) who may be an officer of the Commonwealth for the purposes of this Act in respect of the business or undertaking described in that subsection; or

(b) the circumstances in which a parliamentarian may be an officer of a person conducting a business or undertaking for the purposes of this Act" (*Work Health and Safety Act 2011*, Austl., s.247).

Public Authority

Concerning the term *officer* as a Public Authority;

"A person who makes, or participates in making, decisions that affect the whole, or a substantial part, of the business or undertaking of a public authority is taken to be an officer of the public authority for the purposes of this Act" (*Work Health and Safety Act 2011*, Austl., s.252).

Definition

An officer, in a broad sense, is anyone who works for the PCBU officially or otherwise, and whose work significantly affects the PCBU through the decision-making process that in turn affects a whole or part of the PCBU.

To clarify a Safety Officer or Adviser is not usually an Officer under this definition. However, if they can directly or indirectly affect the workplace and affect it in a significant manner, they may be considered an officer. It depends on their roles and responsibilities in contract or by arrangement.

Reasonable person

A reasonable person is an objective term that can be tested by several qualities. While the actual tests are strict and involve knowledge of many common law and negligence cases, some understanding of the concept can be established. It is a term used to describe what a reasonable person would do in a given situation. The reasonable person is hypothetical and cannot be called to witness or engage as a person. It is a term that has been defined through common law cases. It is usually but not always associated with determining negligence. A reasonable person's qualities are likely to be determined by the appraisal of the;

1.) Knowledge relevant to the workplace and its hazards
2.) Likelihood of harm, injury or damage
3.) Role within the organisation
4.) Skills and available resources

    5.) Qualifications

    6.) Information processed

    7.) Awareness of consequences should the WHS system fail

In addition to these factors, the UK identified that regulated positions should be occupied by those who are fit and proper. In defining the fit and proper person the characteristics are:

1.) **Good Character**: This involves assessing the integrity, honesty, and reliability of the individual. The person's behaviour and past actions must reflect a good character, especially when they are in a position of trust.

2.) **Qualifications**: The individual should possess the necessary educational background, certifications, or licenses required for the role. This ensures that they have the formal training and knowledge base pertinent to their responsibilities.

3.) **Competence**: This refers to the person's ability to perform their job effectively. It includes having the right level of understanding, skill, and judgment to carry out the tasks associated with their role12.

4.) **Skills and Experience**: The individual should have the practical skills and experience relevant to the role they are performing. This includes both the technical skills required for the job and the soft skills necessary for interacting with others and managing situations.

5.) **Health**: The person must be physically and mentally capable of performing the tasks that are intrinsic to their role, with reasonable adjustments made if

necessary (*The Health and Social Care Act 2008
(Regulated Activities) Regulations 2014*, UK).

It would be expected that a prudent reasonable person,
would have the above characteristics and be considered fit
and proper for the position that they undertake. It should be
noted that the reasonable person is a dynamic yet objective
standard. Meaning that it will vary with the position and
qualities of the person involved, but will remain objective in
its appraisal. A reasonable doctor, lawyer, manager etc can
be used as a variation to the dynamics of the objective test.
Furthermore, this universal term is found in common law
throughout the Australian states and beyond.

Due Diligence

Due diligence can be likened to a level or standard of
governance that an officer should have over certain WHS
matters. In harmonised legislation, it is usually section 27 of
the corresponding Acts that deal with Due Diligence. Due
diligence commonly entails;

1.) Acquiring Knowledge

Knowledge of the businesses Safety and Health matters.

2.) Understanding Operations

Understanding the nature of operations and its related
hazards.

3.) Resource Utilization

Being able to use resources effectively to mitigate risks.

4.) Information

Information, consultation and cooperation is facilitated.

5.) Compliance Processes

Compliance to the laws and duties is achieved.

6.) Verification

To have verified proof that resources and process are being used to minimise risks and that the officer and PCBU are compliant to their duties of due diligence (*Work Health and Safety Act 2020*, W.A.).

In Victorian legislation under section 26 *Duties of persons who manage or control workplaces*, the persons managing an employer's assets and resources etc are treated in a different manner than Officers in other state or territory legislation.

"(1) A person who (whether as an owner or otherwise) has, to any extent, the management or control of a workplace must ensure so far as is reasonably practicable that the workplace and the means of entering and leaving it are safe and without risks to health.

(2) The duties of a person under subsection (1) apply only in relation to matters over which the person has management

or control"(*Occupational Health and Safety Act 2004*, Vic., s.26)
.

The standard of care is not doubled up in Victorian legislation through a statement of Due Diligence. Instead, it places the well tested Duty of Care on the entire chain of effect from directors, designers, suppliers, fitters and workers etc the standard of care is given by what a reasonable person would do so far as it is reasonably practicable.

There are other Victorian laws that determine a duty of due diligence that impact safety. These laws although not altogether part of the safety regulations may apply in terms of home and land sales and building structures. However, the term due diligence is not used in Victorian occupational safety and health legislation. Also, Victorian legislation may use the term reckless endangerment to cover similar areas as due diligence.

Therefore, due diligence in a broad sense is still part of the WHS system requirements Australia wide, whether it is literally written into legislation or not. The Duty of Due diligence is to ensure that the resources and processes are verifiably used to mitigate risks at the workplace. In determining if the duty of due diligence has been met, 6 criteria are required. Knowledge of the Safety and Health Matters, Understanding the nature of the workplace hazards, Utilising resources to mitigate risks and treat hazards, Information is shared throughout the organisation, Compliance to standards exists and Verification of the resources and processes mitigating the risks also exist.

Reasonably Practicable

The terms reasonably practical and reasonably practicable are slightly different terms. Reasonably practicable is used as part of describing the onus of the Duty of Care in all states and territories. The difference is that the term practicable implies both practical and able. In other words, it is as practical and able. Whereas the term practical does not have intrinsically by definition a limitation.

At any given time reasonably practicable, concerning health and safety, means taking into account and weighing up all relevant factors such as;

1. "...the likelihood of the hazard or the risk concerned occurring; and
2. the likelihood of the hazard or the risk concerned occurring; the degree of harm that might result from the hazard or the risk; and
3. what the person concerned knows, or ought reasonably to know, about —
     (i) and the hazard or the risk; and
     (ii) ways of eliminating or minimising the risk; and
4. the availability and suitability of ways to eliminate or minimise the risk; and
5. after assessing the extent of the risk and the available ways of eliminating or minimising the risk, the cost associated with available ways of eliminating or minimising the risk, including whether the cost is grossly disproportionate to the risk..." (*Work Health and Safety Act 2020*, W.A.).

In a broader sense the following aspects need to always be considered when determining a reasonably practicable:

6. The likelihood of the hazard or the risk concerned occurring.

The higher the chances the more foreseeable the circumstance and hence the greater the significance of the event.

7. Degree of harm that may result if the hazard or risk eventuated

The higher the amount of harm or damage the more weight is given towards arguments of negligence. Therefore, the higher the probable damage or harm the more significant the event.

8. What the person concerned knows, or ought reasonably to know, about the hazard or risk and any ways of eliminating or minimising the risk

The state of knowledge is concerned with what a person knows in comparison to what others in equivalent positions would know. The underlying purpose of the knowledge is to be able to identify and treat the risks, and potential harm and damage.

9. Availability and suitability of ways to eliminate or minimise risks

Ways to eliminate or minimise the risk are established using the hierarchy of controls.

10. Cost of eliminating or minimising the risk

The cost of eliminating and minimising the risk is the last item to weigh up in the process as it determines to cost feasibility of mitigating the risk under a proposed plan. This would be a cost-benefit analysis between the risk value and the amount reduced through the fiscal plan and its cost (*Interpretive Guideline – Model Work Health And Safety Act The Meaning Of 'Reasonably Practicable'*, Austl.).

Negligence

In a broad sense, Negligence means not taking care of something that otherwise we would expect a reasonable person to take care of. In occupational health and safety, the term is used to refer to the reasonably practical person not exercising their duty of care. Neglect and negligence are a little different. Neglect simply means not caring for someone or something. It is the act of neglecting. Negligence is more than neglect it is a legal statement that certain reasonable actions or omissions that were expected did not occur and this led to consequences that are being faced or have been faced. To determine if negligence has occurred is a complex process that requires specialised knowledge usually held by high-level lawyers, barristers and judges. Also, negligence is defined by the body of the law. The body of the law refers to the law derived from the common law cases. This means it is very difficult to write a specific definition for the term without elaborating and bringing up in detail common law cases.

Duty of Care

In a broad sense, Negligence is usually established when certain criteria are met. Firstly, there needs to be a duty of care between the two parties. More parties can be involved, but negligence is a personal onus to care for another directly so that no matter how many parties there are the onus may be between all parties to each other. In most cases proving a duty of care is the first step in establishing a negligence case.

Breach of Duty

Secondly. There needs to be proof that the duty of care was not exercised or not adequately. This can be a statutory breach of the duty of care or otherwise. Thirdly, an injury or damage must have resulted from the event. Then lastly it must be proven that the actions or events under question were related to the duty of care, by determining causation.

When assessing a breach in the duty of care, also known as the standard of care, standards, reasonability, probability, severity and cost are some of the things that affect the decision. Once the Duty of Care is established the next point of interest is whether there was a breach of the duty or it was not exercised so far as is reasonably practicable.

Harm or Injury

A harm must have occurred leading to injury. Injury and Damage are usually assessed financially or through the use of scheduled tables throughout the Australian State legislation. A no fault compensation system is setup throughout Australia meaning that harm or injury occurring at work is deemed compensable. Negligence does not need to be proven unless common law action is undertaken. Not all jurisdictions permit common law proceedings in the courts. An example comparison as at Oct 2021 demonstrates some differences and similarities between the various compensatory systems;

Table 26

Compensation systems by State

State / Territory	Benefit Type	Maximum Amount	Access to Common law
A.C.T.	No Lump sum	$158,964 (Single) $238,466 (Multiple)	N.A
N.S.W	Permanent impairment compensation *Workers Compensation Act 1987* (N.S.W), s.66. Some workers exempt	Variable by date of accident. Pain and suffering not payable except for exempt workers	Thresholds exist for access to lump sum payments
N.T.	Lump Sum	$351,582.40 S.71	N.A.
Qld.	Standard Additional 30% or greater DPI (s192(2)) Gratuitous care (s193(6))	• 216.15 times QOTE (standard) • 216.15 times QOTE	Prescribed levels depending on DPI and other factors based on prescribed amounts

	Additional particular workers (s193A(2)) Latent onset (s128B), Workers' Compensation and Rehabilitation Act 2003 (Qld).	(additional — s192(2)) • 244.86 times QOTE (Gratuitous care) • $36,190 (additional — s193A(2)) • 453.92 times QOTE (Latent onset)	(s.192), (s.193), (s.193A).
S.A.	Lump Sum Options 1. 5% WPI, No Economic Loss 2. 5-29% WPI, Economic loss 3. 30% Income support till retired	$502,620 (non-economic loss) $390,502.00 (economic loss)	30% WPI required for access to common law damages (*Return to work Act 2014, (S.A.), s.72*)
Tas.	Lump Sum	$396,001.30	20% Threshold Whole person impairment. *Workers Rehabilitation and Compensation Act 1988*, (Tas.), s.138AB.
Vic.	Combined Lump Sum and payments	$644,640 — s217, Workplace Injury Rehabilitation	

		and Compensation Act 2013 (Vic.).	
W.A.	Lump sum for single or multiple impairments, *Workers' Compensation and Injury Management Act 1981* (WA).	$239,179 for Schedule 2 impairments	Common law: not less than 15% WPI (limited damages) and not less than 25% WPI (unlimited damages) Other criteria exist that can be used.

(adapted from All State and Commonwealth Compensation Legislation, CCH, 2024a; Safe Work Australia, 2024d)

QOTE = Queensland Original Time Earnings

WPI = Whole person impairment

DPI = Degree of permanent impairment

From these various compensation systems, we can infer that whole person's impairment and the degree of permanent impairment are seen as significant factors in determining the severity of the harm or injury. Broadly speaking, an individual with high whole person impairment that is the whole function of the person is impaired significantly, then the more options available to them throughout Australia. However, it should be noted that common law claims are handled differently and in some the access is limited while in other eliminated.

Causation

Causation determines if the cause of the harm was in fact because of something the defendant did or omitted. Often it is referred to as a factual cause. Usually, proximate cause describes the situation when the causation of the harm, in all fairness, policy and practicality, the defendant can be considered legally accountable for the harm (Owen, 2007).

Causation the last of the four points in determining negligence has also many variables to consider including the "But For" test, proximity, eggshell principle, mitigation and Nova actus interviniens (New Intervening Act).

But For Test

Firstly the "But for" test means that if it were not for the actions or omissions the effect would not have been existent or realised to the extent it was (Coady, 2002).

Proximity

Secondly, proximity or a relationship must exist prior to the duty of care being established. The proximity of those who buy a product with the manufacturer for instance was considered a proximity issue. Donoghue v. Stevenson established that proximity existed between a ginger beer customer and the manufacturer. Proximity included a neighbourly nature to the duty of care. Ever since those initial developments proximity has changed considerably (Derrington, 1991; *Donoghue v Stevenson*, 1932).

Eggshell principle

Thirdly, to help determine the proximity of the relationship often the eggshell principle was used. Traditionally it meant to take your victim as you find them. So that it could not be argued that a person had weak bones and therefore they broke due to the incident. This in turn brought a significant number of cases into a proximal relationship. It protected all people with a disability and those whom were more fragile than others (Jones, 2001).

Mitigation

Mitigation means the injured party had made reasonable steps to avoid injury and that the actions of a reasonable and foreseeable nature applied. When determining damages it plays the effect of limiting the injured party from recovering the damages that could have been avoided through reasonable efforts (Adar, 2012). It has been argued that the concept of Mitigation has led to a form of Comparative negligence instead of Contributory negligence. It has taken the place of Contributory negligence over the years. Contributory negligence is slightly different in that it does not look at the reasonable avoidance of injury but rather the contributory actions of negligence. They are slightly different but both affect the damages that can be claimed. It should be noted that most Western nations no longer consider Contributory negligence while most consider Comparative negligence through mitigation (Adar, 2012).

Novus Actus Interveniens (New Intervening Act)

As part of determining causation for negligence, there needs to be a new foreseeable act that caused the harm. However, novus actus interviniens is said to arise when the new act breaks or intervenes with the chain connecting the wrongdoing and the person harmed. This could mean the involvement of a third party, rescuer, natural disasters or some other event that caused the intervention. It is a complex principle that in itself could be broken down to a number of constituent legal principles. However, the purpose here is to highlight that while a new foreseeable act causing the harm is imperative to establishing negligence. There are a few factors such as exasperation and reoccurring new incidents that can be considered valid arguments towards negligence. But in some cases where for example there were mechanisms to maintain a floor condition in a usable state, but negligence had led to a spill of oil on the floor, then a flood arises from rain as a novus actus interviniens washing the oil away, then an injury occurred from slipping on the floor. Depending on the variables and what actually took place it could be argued that the novus actus interviniens intercepted the chain leading to the injury (Adelaide Law Review, 1963).

Precedence

The doctrine of Precedence is a term used to describe an interpretation of the law based on what has been decided in the past for similar cases. There are two types of precedence

i. Binding Precedence

Binding precedence is bound to the court level and type such as a high court decision affecting only other High court decisions.

ii. Persuasive Precedence

Persuasive precedence affects all court levels but is not binding.

Further Reading

Adar, Y. (2012). *Comparative Negligence and Mitigation of Damages: Two Doctrines in Search of Reunion.* https://papers.ssrn.com/sol3/papers.cfm?abstract_id=2078874

Adelaide Law Review. (1963). Negligence: Novus actus interveniens - rescuer killed by negligence of third party - apportionment of liability - contributory negligence of rescuer. *The Adelaide Law Review, 10*(2), 112.

Caparo Industries plc v Dickman [1990] 2 AC 605.

CCH. (2024a). *Australian Workers Compensation Commentary.* CCH IntelliConnect.

Coady, D. A. (2002). Testing for Causation in Tort Law. *Australian Journal of Legal Philosophy, 3*(27), 83. https://classic.austlii.edu.au/au/journals/AUJlLegPhil/2002/3.pdf

Connelly v RTZ Corporation Plc and Others [1997] UKHL 30. http://www.bailii.org/uk/cases/UKHL/1997/30.html

Corporations Act 2001. (Austl.). Retrieved from https://www.legislation.gov.au/Details/C2022C00306

Derrington, J. (1991). Proximity, the Standard of Care and Damage - Relating the Elements of Negligence. *University of Queensland Law Journal, 16*(2), 272.

Donoghue v Stevenson [1932] UKHL 100. https://www.bailii.org/

Grant v Australian Knitting Mills [1936] SASR 113. https://www.austlii.edu.au/

Hamilton v Nuroof (WA) Pty Ltd [1956] HCA 42.

The Health and Social Care Act 2008 (Regulated Activities) Regulations 2014. (UK). Retrieved from https://www.legislation.gov.uk/uksi/2014/2936/regulation/19/made

Interpretive Guideline – Model Work Health And Safety Act The Meaning Of 'Reasonably Practicable'. (Austl.).

Jones, T. (2001). The Commonwealth v W L McLean: Developments Inconsistent with the Traditional Nature of the Egg Shell Skull Principle. *James Cook University Law Review*(8), 78.

Labour Hire Licensing Act 2018. (Vic.). Retrieved from https://www.legislation.vic.gov.au/

Latimer v AEC Ltd [1953] UKHL 3. http://www.bailii.org/uk/cases/UKHL/1953/3.html

Model Work Health and Safety Act 2011. (Austl.).

Model Work Health and Safety Bill 2022. (Austl.).

Occupational Health and Safety Act 2004. (Vic.).

Owen, D. G. (2007). The Five Elements of Negligence. *Hofstra Law Review*, 35(4), 1671.

Paris v Stepney BC [1951] AC 367. https://www.bailii.org/uk/cases/UKHL/1950/3.html

Safe Work Australia. (2024d). *Table 5.6: Common law provisions | Safe Work Australia*. Safe Work Australia. https://www.safeworkaustralia.gov.au/book/compariso n-workers-compensation-arrangements-australia-and-new-zealand-2021-28th-edition/chapter-5-benefits/table-56-common-law-provisions

Smith v Charles Baker & Sons [1891] UKHL 2. https://www.bailii.org/uk/cases/UKHL/1891/2.html

Stone v Bolton [1951] AC 850.

Watt v Hertfordshire County Council [1954] EWCA 6. http://www.bailii.org/ew/cases/EWCA/Civ/1954/6.ht ml

Wilsons & Clyde Coal Co v English [1938] AC 57. https://www.bailii.org/

Work Health and Safety Act 2011. (Austl.).

Work Health and Safety Act 2020. (W.A.).

Statistical Model

When developing a statistical model, the model needs to have both lead and lag indicators. The difference between the two can an time be somewhat unclear. A lead indicator is defined as a measurable or observable variable that predicts a change or movement in another data series, process, trend, or other phenomenon of interest before it occurs. A lag indicator is an observable or measurable factor that changes sometime after the economic, financial, or business variable with which it is correlated changes (Reiff, 2023).

In some instances, data can be proactive and a lead indicator while other times it may be a reactive lag indicator. For example, compliance audits maybe used to set up risk defences and their value is seen as a lead indicator. Compliance post incident would check to see if something in the defences or level of compliance had caused the incident. Such would be a reactive use of compliance data and is considered a lag indicator.

The statistical model presented here aims to provide a basic coverage of the Duty of Care and Due Diligence. Numerous roles and responsibilities will apply to the attainment of the statistics required. A minimal duty of care requires the collection of data and using the data in an appropriate manner. It is an indirect requirement for the standard of care we know as the duty of care.

Duty of Care Data

The following qualities of the Duty of care also involve data collection, handling, storage and disposal. Firstly, the data collected must correspond to the Duty of Care and its standards i.e.;

1. Providing and maintaining a healthy and safe work environment
2. Providing and maintaining safe plant and structures
3. Provision and maintenance of safe systems of work
4. Ensuring the safe use, handling and storage of plant, structures and substances
5. Provision of adequate facilities for the welfare of workers
6. Information, training, instruction or supervision to perform work
7. Monitoring to ensure workplace conditions (*Model Work Health and Safety Act 2011*, Austl.).

The workplace health and safety work environment can be captured using several lead and lag indicators. Statically it can be assessed by the use of inspections and suitable inspection checklists. Alternatively, supervision of the workplace may involve supervisory-level orders or actions that require documentation.

Plant and equipment when designed, supplied, installed and operated must have documentation that the design is in compliance with relative standards and that it has appropriate guards and safety-engineered aspects. The supply is done safely, using correct labelling on substances, transport codes and other transport safety requirements. The installation process is thought out and installed to minimise risks. Clearance documents such as commissioning orders, isolation tags and so forth all require documentation. Furthermore, some plant under regulations variable by state will require registration with the Regulator of that state.

Providing and maintaining safe systems of work means that some jobs will require a procedure to follow. It is an administrative way of dealing with known hazards. Documentation may include the selection of the job to be analysed, the job task analysis, job safety analysis (the safety aspects of the job task analysis), risks and hazards treatment and workarounds, safe work method policy, plan and procedures.

Safe use, handling and storage of plant structures and substances. Each one of these points is a large field of application. Safe use and handling incorporate the previous points on a job analysis and using job safety analysis to investigate a task set safe working procedures and make treatments to any risks. Storage will depend on many things it is a substance labelling, isolation by distance, bunting, safe storage, reagent isolation and avoidance and much more to do with substance safety can be established. Each of these aspects can be documented such as the process of taking an item or resource and storing it can be managed using a resource management system. If the item is maintainable or has an expiry then these should also be documented. For example, bullets that have been in storage for a long time may do one of three things, remain stable, deteriorate or become volatile. Each possibility comes with a set of conditions that need to be met the biggest culprit for volatile and deteriorated ammo is temperature. Most bullets are capable of lasting ten years but it depends on many variables, such as temperature, moisture, pressure (physical damage) and generally age. Therefore, in those circumstances, careful documentation of resource allocation, handling and storage is important to maintain safe ammunition.

Adequate facilities for workers may include the documentation of provisions and rations such as a bottle of water at the beginning of a shift and or throughout a shift. The bottle of water may be rationed on a checklist to determine who has and hasn't received, or how many each person received. Alternatively, the provision of static supplies can be inspected and hence documenting that they are maintained.

Information, training, instruction or supervision to perform work safely may involve multiple records and data. Information in the form of emails, texts and other forms of correspondence should be in part documented against the criteria to do a job safely. This means all information to do with safety should be as well documented as possible. Similar to the stringent accounting controls for finances. Informational data includes qualitative information from consultation and correspondence, this is usually stored in the original format that it was sent. However, in some workplaces especially some government departments, there is a register of incoming and outgoing calls and the reason for the call. There is also a permanent record of any queries formally handled by such departments. While it would be impractical to commit resources to managing the documentation of information, correspondence and consultation, some aspects can be captured for the sake of safety. This system involves the use of site diaries. In construction where hundreds of calls and consultations may occur in a given hour, the best way to handle these situations is to use a diary for all safety-related information transfer. Inspection requests, isolation tag pre-removal inspections, unsafe condition alerts and so forth. This ensures that as the dynamics of the workplace change, the workers are informed adequately of existing and changing conditions to do their jobs safely.

Training, Instruction and or supervision are all related to the previous point. Information data establishes over time a platform for what needs to be trained. In addition, many inputs will establish training requirements and these require documentation. So, if the question was asked "Was the training adequate?", it can be proved to be based on documented experience. Instruction and supervision likewise need to document the actions of supervisors, their time on a shift, their location, the team they are supervising and data to handle what they are experiencing on site regarding safety. It must be communicated and consulted throughout the shift. It is not the case that people are trained and therefore no supervision is required. Although the statutes may lead one to believe so, the common law requires as a minimum the information, resources and supervision to be present. If supervision is not done immediately within the vicinity, it may be done from a distance, however, the purpose of supervision is to allow a person with experience to gauge a situation and relay the information to those with less experience. Eliminating supervision is taking away Information or the ability to inform those who have already been trained and instructed. There is a trend in the workplaces to try and eliminate leading hands and supervisory roles, but if careful selection is made, the person in such a position can effectively increase the quality of the safety systems in place.

Finally, the last point is to maintain workplace conditions through monitoring. Video monitoring can involve video evidence that is documented by recording incidents and saving them. Although most monitoring systems have a lifetime cycle of approximately a week or two weeks. This means that the same storage space is re-used and old footage is replaced by new footage once a week or within a fortnight. On larger more professional systems the cycle is monthly or more. Video monitoring with a person monitoring the screen is used in some places. They further document the time location and incidents as they unravel. Incidents may be changes in the workplace that cause unsafe conditions or increase risks to safety. The overall process of monitoring can come with monthly inspection checklist data for various systematic components. Monitored items on the checklist may include, emergency pathways and systems, firefighting capacity, consultation and communication system checks, isolated worker checks, confined space occurrences (sometimes confined spaces are created dynamically), dispute resolution checks etc.

All the factors mentioned for the duty of care will be elaborated further under the section for performance indicators. This introduction to the data required is a guide and not a reference. When auditing for example vast amounts of documents is used in the process, it is beyond the scope of this book to elaborate in detail every possible data and document that can be used as proof. However, the duty of care is only one side of things, as an organisation and as officers' due diligence also has a set of requirements that need to be met.

Due Diligence Data

The due diligence information and data that require collection and processing include the following qualities.

1. Knowledge
2. Nature of hazards and work
3. Resources
4. Instruction, information and consultation
5. Compliance
6. Verify, Check and Review (*Model Work Health and Safety Act 2011*, Austl.).

Knowledge means that there is data to and fro in the form of correspondence documented in diaries and schedules. In some organisations, it may be difficult to capture the details of every consultation or conversation. However, diary entries for milestones or significant changes in the workplace require documentation. Having said that some surprises occur that are after-the-fact entries into diaries. Which is ok, as long as it is stated what happened and when. The next important matter is that it should be highlighted that the correspondence is for process documentation. "Hi I am calling or writing to document a situation or incident" and the situation is then documented. This ensures that the information shared daily is not shielded which is what managers were taught to do. Shielding and isolation mean limiting the number of interferences usually through an administration desk and restricting who has access to the manager's or officer's contact details. This is supposedly done to enhance productivity and focus. An officer needs to know that the information is relevant to safety and that it is important enough to document. There is usually no point in communicating "a truck has arrived". "What are the safety concerns?" "What is different to any other truck or vehicle that has arrived?" All these and many more questions and variables can impact the dynamic shift of knowledge. Therefore, it is important to communicate and highlight their significance.

Static knowledge is also important and this type is usually preserved as a qualification, certificate or some other form of merit document acknowledging the knowledge of the individual. Training and other formal training data can also be used to justify that the officer knew the work being done. Knowledge of this form is considered an assurance. More will be detailed on assurance; however, it is worth noting that assurance raises confidence in the ability to perform.

Knowing about the nature of the hazards at the workplace usually involves a risk register. More information will be provided on this matter. However, for clarity risk and hazard registers offer a static form of documenting a risk and or hazard. Note that risk management begins with identification of the risk and the register usually contains information for the identification process and some include other parts of the treatment process.

Resources cover a wide range of things such as documenting the; provision of PPE, and the allocation of manpower and equipment needed to do the job safely. Resource allocation registers or resource management systems are often used.

Instruction, Information and consultation may involve collecting prestart meeting data, ensuring a consultative process during prestart and the shift through issue and dispute resolution process documentation.

Compliance surveys, inspections and audit data can be used to establish compliance issues. Work orders, risk treatment information and resource allocations towards compliance can also be documented.

Verification, checking and reviewing can be done through ongoing monitoring data, audits, meeting information and date and survey information. Consultative feedback data and corrective action data would be used as part of the verification process.

The statistical model described so far is complex as it has at the backend of its interface, several different data sources and treatments. These data sources can be categorised into performance indicators which will be used to make a statement of position and a statement of performance. The statement of position includes the current status of the variables and data sources described. The statement of position can be summed up with the question: "Where are we positioned?". The statement of performance on the other hand looks at the same or different variables and data sources over time. It is defined by the questions "What have we done and how well?"(O'Neill & Wolfe, 2017).

Performance Indicators

Injury and Disease Data

Injury and disease data were possibly the first statistics required by all organisations to develop. The reports would state where the injury or disease levels are and the performance would identify trends with the statistics. Historically, it was one of the principal statistics to maintain.

There are several different statistics reported normally in all Australian States:

1. The number of deaths
2. The number of injuries and disease onsets
3. Lost Time Incident Frequency Rate
4. Incident Rate
5. Average Time Lost Rate

Incident Rate (IR):

$$IR = \frac{Number\ of\ incidents\ in\ the\ period}{Number\ of\ workers} \times 100$$

(CCH, 1991)

Frequency Rate (FR):

$$FR = \frac{Number\ of\ incidents\ in\ the\ period}{Total\ number\ of\ hours\ worked\ in\ the\ period} \times 1,000,000$$

(CCH, 1991; O'Neill & Wolfe, 2017)

The formula can be used for calculating the Lost Time Injury Frequency rate by placing the number of LTI's in the numerator. The Total hours worked in the period is usually a statistic tied to payroll and or human resources. That is to say that the total hours worked are marked by the total hours paid for in payroll as total ordinary hours.

For other incidents, the same formula can be used replacing the term incident with the desired incident type. Such as the Vehicle collision frequency rate would have the number of vehicle collisions in the numerator. Keep in mind that the total hours worked is organisation-wide and may be better specified as subsidiary or workgroup total hours worked.

Total Incident Frequency Rate (TIFR):

Also known as Total Incident Rate (TIR).

$$TIR = \frac{Total\ number\ of\ incidents\ in\ the\ period}{Total\ number\ of\ hours\ worked\ in\ the\ period} \times 1,000,000$$

(CCH, 1991; O'Neill & Wolfe, 2017)

This is an alternative to the Frequency Rate. The Total number of incidents takes into account all incidents not just one category such as LTI's. In other places in the world, it is multiplied by 200,000 instead of 1,000,000. Throughout Australia, it is multiplied by 1,000,000.

Average Time Lost Rate: (ATLR):

$$ATLR = \frac{Number\ of\ working\ days\ lost}{Number\ of\ occurrences\ in\ the\ period}$$

(CCH, 1991)

As a minimum, the collection of enough information to calculate the preceding statistics is needed by most organisations. In some organisations there is a visible decline in LTI, however, in others or the same organisation years later, the LTIFr will plateau. So that it doesn't seem to change much over time. At that plateau point, the LTIFR gives less visual indication of performance. Also, although a good indicator of performance it is not the only indicator and other indicators need to be considered also.

Additional data could supplement these Injury and Disease statistics. For example, the collection of health data related to first aid data, air quality, worker exposure levels, and health status of airways. Similarly, noise, vibration measurements of the workplace and doses by workers along with hearing tests etc. allow injury and disease data to be collected treated and monitored.

Compensation Data

Compensation data has a greater variation per State. Some of these differences are highlighted by the different legislation used by each State (Safe Work Australia, 2023b). However, if the criteria that the injury occurred in the workplace, was work-related and there was an injury are met, then generally an application for workers compensation can be made. While negligence does not need to be present in some jurisdictions proving it can open a doorway to common law proceedings. The employer usually accepts a fault-free obligation to assist with the insurer any person injured at work and while doing what they were meant to be doing.

Worker personal data regarding the qualities of a reasonable person, such as qualifications, experience, knowledge of the processes etc can be documented. This will aid the situation if compensation is claimed. In addition, employment records of times and dates worked are important to keep as these will be used to calculate the rate of compensation payments as well as any injury statistic like an LTI. In addition, all workers' compensation data must be kept for 7 years (CCH, 2024b). Therefore, an archive system will also be needed.

Key performance indicators can include the previously mentioned data such as comparisons between experience, qualifications and skills vs compensation claims. In addition to those mentioned, absenteeism, job satisfaction, market job value, employment type (e.g. Full-time, Part-time and Casual), transiency of the workforce and wage gaps etc. can be collected.

Table 27

If injuries during travel to and from work are covered by the jurisdictional compensation scheme?

Jurisdiction	Covered?
Australian Capital Territory	✓
Commonwealth	✗
Commonwealth Seafarers	✓
New South Wales	✓
Northern Territory	✓
Queensland	✓
South Australia	✗
Tasmania	✗
Victoria	✗
Western Australia	✗

(CCH, 2024b)

Some differences in compensation data stored by each jurisdiction will vary across the Australian States.

Incident Data

Data collected in all the States of Australia conform to relevant standards and to the requirements of the regulators (Safe Work Australia, 2015; Standards Australia, 1990). Most States ask the same or similar set of questions such as;

"What happened?", "When did it happen?", Where did it happen?", What happened in detail?", Who did it happen to?", "How and where are they being treated?", "Who is the PCBU or Mine operator or work provider?", "What is being done at the time of reporting?" "Who is notifying?"(Worksafe (WA), 2023). Also, in mines, you may need to provide the mine and operator names and locations.

In describing what happened during an incident the question "why did it happen"? may arise. This then commits data for root causes. In addition, every incident is evaluated to determine if it is notifiable or reportable to the regulator. Victoria may vary the requirement in the near future so the duty to notify is not only for the PCBU, employer or provider but also for the operator of certain plant and equipment. This variation was planned for July 2024.

Duty to notify

In all states and territories, the general rule is that an incident is notifiable when there is;

1. "...the death of a person
2. a serious injury or illness, or
3. a dangerous incident ..." (*Model Work Health and Safety Act 2011*, Austl.).

Incident sites are preserved during these events and the regulator initiates actions or instructions thereafter. In some cases, it is difficult to determine if an incident is serious or a situation is dangerous. Guidelines exist for each State and territory through the jurisdictional regulator. The general rule is that if someone stays in the hospital for any period as an inpatient, there is a treatable injury such as amputation or very serious injury to the body. Medical treatment within 48 hours also is notifiable.

In addition, illnesses such as those with a detrimental impact on health can also be notifiable or reportable. This includes any infection related to carrying out work;

1. "...with micro-organisms,
2. that involves providing treatment or care to a person,
3. that involves contact with human blood or body, substances,
4. that involves handling or contact with animals, animal hides, skins, wool or hair, animal carcasses or animal waste products..." (*Work Health and Safety (General) Regulations 2022*, W.A., s.699.a).

At the time of writing and concerning certain zoonoses occurrences in the workplace, the following are notifiable or reportable to the corresponding regulators;

1. "Q fever
2. Anthrax
3. Leptospirosis
4. Brucellosis
5. Hendra Virus
6. Avian Influenza
7. Psittacosis" (*Work Health and Safety (General) Regulations 2022, W.A., s.699.b*)

These prescribed notifiable diseases and zoonoses may change over the years, however, their appearance in legislation predates harmonized laws and has been a consistent entity of the law. In addition, other government agencies unrelated to workplace health and safety also require specific notifications of diseases, this may be initiated through a general practitioner to the fisheries department. In any case the performance indicators we can use are many, including the number of notified incidents, the categorisation of those incidents, such as serious, medically treated, hospitalisation needed, health data etc.

Overall we can categorise some specific performance data needed into various headings, Personal information, Basis of employment, Shift information, Job title and details, Incident information, Outcome of incident, Root Cause, Exposure levels, Severity of Incident etc (Standards Australia, 1990).

Risk and Hazard Register Data

A risk register contains a minimal amount of information regarding the risks found in the workplace. Each broad workplace or workgroup can have several categoric risk registers. For example, hazardous substances, mobile cranes, elevated work platform risk registers etc. Also note that a Hazardous substances register can be a part of the risk register provided that hazardous substance information, SDS and other relevant details are kept.

The risk register itself would contain fields to be filled by relevant personnel. Note some places use a hazard register while others focus on a risk register, they are different yet contain similar information. Such as;

1.) The hazard or risk title
2.) Consequence
3.) Likelihood
4.) Risk level
5.) Controls in place
6.) Controls required
7.) Actioned By
8.) Date Due
9.) Team to deploy
10.) Date completed
11.) Maintenance required
12.) Review date
13.) Monitoring cycle
14.) Verification

(adapted from Safe Work Australia, 2020)

Due Diligence

The risk register is essential to proving the knowledge that a risk or hazard was known and attempts to control it were made. It also identifies the nature of the hazard, but this is dealt with more through a report on the hazard or risk.

Prestart and Consultative Process Data

One of the most important consultative steps is the prestart meeting also known as a hand-over meeting. The process usually entails a leader delivering an operational plan or schedule to the team and the team then asking several questions until everyone is confident in starting their task. Work Health and Safety issues are also raised at handover or prestart meetings. These issues initiate a consultative process.

As discussed regarding the Duty of Due Diligence, all states require a consultative process. The start of a shift or job is the best possible time to convey information regarding safety health and operations. Prestarts usually have an attendance record but there is no reason why it can't be elaborated on, with additional performance criteria. Such as the number of WHS issues raised, what were the issues concerning? If what is being raised is a hazard or risk then it will need to be dealt with through the standard procedure for treating or dealing with risks and hazards.

In the absence of a Health and Safety Committee, the consultative process can be documented similarly. For operational meetings that involve WHS issues, there should be a process for both issue resolution and risk or hazard management to arise. The consultative process integrates with the risk register and issue resolution data. Most of the Prestart and Consultative data is usually qualitative and requires a qualitative approach to deal with such data.

Duty of Care and Due Diligence

The strict statutory definition of the duty of due diligence requires specific information and a consultation process (*Model Work Health and Safety Act 2011*, Austl.). This is intended to enable informed decisions to be made. Also, most of its defining elements are indirectly dependent on a transparent consultative process. In addition, the duty of care specifically requires the consultative process to exist and be functional.

The consultative process helps with all aspects of attempting to control hazards and risks found or identified in the risk register. It complements the entire management system also.

Survey, Inspections and Audit Data

Survey data, inspection data and Audit data can be lead or lag-based. It can be lead-based such as the number of inspections per day as a statistic in comparison with other performance indicators such as behavioural interventions. Survey data can provide important information for the opinions and status of employee satisfaction as well as many other factors.

Surveys

Surveys in more detail can;

- Help identify personnel requirements or preferences
- Identify job-related tasks

- Define and evaluate the work process
- Assess stakeholder or personnel satisfaction, such as identifying or prioritizing issues, risks and hazards.
- Evaluate proposed changes
- Assess whether a change was successful
- Monitor changes in stakeholder or personnel satisfaction over time.
- Qualitative, Quantitative and Semi-qualitative data collection and processing for specific points of interest.

Any WHS statistical model would need to consider the variables identified and assessed through survey data. It will demonstrate a consultative process as well as integrate with other functions and data collected within the statistical model.

Inspections

Often called a walkthrough survey the inspection is more than an identification process. Inspection data aims to usually address compliance against legislation and industry standards. But it also involves identifying and processing information directly related to the work process.

Things that can be dealt with in an inspection include:

- The process
- Number of workers involved
- Materials and substances used, handled and stored
- Controls commissioned and functioning
- Housekeeping
- Environmental conditions such as noise, dust, mists etc

- Appropriate usage of PPE
- Material flow
- Process control records (Temperature, concentration, pressure etc)
- Unreported and sighted near misses and other incidents

(Grantham, 1992)

In a more simplified way of organising things, the inspection is to achieve four primary roles:

- Identify tasks and risks in the work being done
- Appraise the tasks and risks giving them values be it compliance or best practice
- Setting a baseline or benchmark for the next inspection.
- Relay inspection data to integrate with other functions such as consultation, risk register, hazard assessments etc

Tools used during an inspection usually involve a checklist covering the items mentioned or a more specific check. A specific check or inspection isolates a particular task within a job and studies its nature, identifies any risks, documents resources needed to finish the task safely, documents information gained through consultation and establishes the level of compliance of the task or residual risk to statutory and industry requirements.

Audits

Audits achieve a verification, check and review of the systems in place. One could argue that an Audit is similar to an Inspection. The difference is that an Audit attempts to justify and validate both documentation and the work or tasks being conducted.

In a condensed form, it involves an inspection but also tries to cover all aspects of the system in place. There are different Audit types. Audits can focus on

- Overall or Specific Compliance
- Task or Program Specific
- Management System

It is more formal than a general inspection as it involves

- Inspections of the workplaces
- Reviewing the policy, plans and procedures
- Interviewing employees
- Reviewing documentation
- Compliance checking
- Verifying processes

And anything that will provide a clearer picture of the overall system being audited. Also, audits are usually used preceding accreditation to a particular standard.

Compliance Data

While compliance data is attained by surveys, inspections and audits, other contributory sources exist. Compliance data is within itself an area of important concern. The regulators may take into account continual improvement in determining the consequential penalties. However, the regulator only has two basic options to consider, is the subject is compliant or not. The corresponding penalty is a prescribed amount which means it is not flexible until or if it goes to court.

(Due Diligence)

The Statutory definition of Due Diligence requires compliance data to be collected. Each state has different requirements for this dataset. General records to keep include;

1. "Incident Records,
2. Hazardous Substances/Chemicals,
3. Plant Registration Documents,
4. Tests and Inspection Reports" (SafeWork (SA), 2020).
5. "Training Activities,
6. First Aid Treatments,
7. Incident Investigations" (Worksafe (ACT), 2020).

Resources and process data

The resource allocation and functional processes are usually identified by two broad data sets;

1. Establishing, implementing and maintaining a Safety management system
2. Resource allocation for each procedure is documented (Comcare, 2024).

(Due Diligence)

Due diligence requirements include the documentation of the safety management system in terms of policies, plans and procedures. It also includes the process for the management of risks.

Resource allocation to meet the requirements of the policies, plans and procedures is essential to meeting the obligations of due diligence. Client or Resource management systems may be of use in keeping a record of when and where particular resources were used. This may include a sign-in and out register for specific items like the use of harnesses, stretchers, P.P.E. distribution and stocking.

Consultative Feedback Verification Data

The data used during various consultations can be formalised. One specific area of consultation is to verify if the changes, processes, and resources are substantially contributing to a safer workplace. The tools are most often the same as all other areas where review is required. This means that surveys, audits, inspections, meetings, and hazard or risk analysis are the most commonly used tools.

(Due Diligence) – verification process

The verification process to determine consultative feedback has been processed is based on the development and use of existing management tools. The scope should be to review that substantial consultation and the desired quality of that consultation has occurred. In determining the quality of the consultation an officer will need to take into account that there has been effective change or ratification of systems and resources in place.

Data will come in as feedback and consultation forms, meeting minutes, data processing and handling, actions and changes derived from consultations, trust, privacy and integrity of data established etc. Also, there will be integration with corrective action or risk registers.

Verification and Corrective Data

Verification of the management system and the corrective process occurs through what is known as an assurance process. This can be defined by three broad areas where controls need to be assured

1. Technical Control Assurance
2. Cultural Control Assurance
3. Governance Assurance.

Proactive approaches involve collecting data on a regular systematic basis. Usually in the form of Audits, surveys and inspections.

Reactive approaches to assurance involve using historical data such as incident statistics. This helps determine the scope of the plans and changes needed.

(Due Diligence)-verification process

With respect to due diligence all aspects of the duty of due diligence require verification. Therefore, this means collecting data as highlighted under the broader *Due Diligence Data.*

Other Relevant Data

Other areas covered in part elsewhere in the book include Emergency Data, Review Data, Monitoring Data, Safety Meeting Data, Maintenance Data, Training Data and Financial Data. All these aspects are part of the overall assurance of the system at hand.

Also, as a note, the purchasing process may include documentation of codes of practice and Standard conformity. Such as purchasing wheelchairs complying with relevant Australian Standards. The process for procurement in some instances is a WHS matter.

Further Reading

CCH. (1991). *Planning Occupational Safety and Health* (3rd ed.). CCH.

CCH. (2024b). *Obligations around termination of employment (notice and keeping job open).* http://intelliconnect.ezproxy.ecu.edu.au/scion/secure/ct x_10654914/index.jsp?cpid=WKAP-TAL-IC#page[3]

Comcare. (2024). *Guidance for officers in exercising due diligence.* Comcare.

Grantham, D. (1992). *Occupational health and hygiene guidebook for the whso.* D.L. Grantham.

Model Work Health and Safety Act 2011. (Austl.).

O'Neill, S., & Wolfe, K. (2017). *Measuring and reporting on work health and safety.* Safe Work Australia. https://www.safeworkaustralia.gov.au/system/files/doc uments/1802/measuring-and-reporting-on-work-health-and-safety.pdf

Reiff, N. (2023). *Leading Indicators: Definition and How They're Used by Investors.* https://www.investopedia.com/

Safe Work Australia. (2015). *Incident notification fact sheet - Incident-notification-fact-sheet-2015 UD.PDF.* https://www.safeworkaustralia.gov.au/sites/default/file s/2022-09/Incident-notification-fact-sheet-2015%20UD.PDF

Safe Work Australia. (2020). *Template and example COVID-19 risk register.* https://covid19.swa.gov.au/doc/template-and-example-covid-19-risk-register

Safe Work Australia. (2023b). *Comparison of workers compensation arrangements in Australia and New Zealand 29th Edition (2023).* Safe Work Australia. https://www.safeworkaustralia.gov.au/sites/default/file s/2024-04/comparison_of_workers_compensation_arrangements_ in_australia_and_new_zealand_29th_edition_2023.pdf

SafeWork (SA). (2020, 2020-11-10). *Keeping records | SafeWork SA.* SafeWork (S.A.). https://www.safework.sa.gov.au/resources/simple-steps-to-safety/keeping-records

Standards Australia. (1990). *Workplace injury and disease recording standard (AS 1885.1 1990).*

Work Health and Safety (General) Regulations 2022. (W.A.).

Worksafe (ACT). (2020, 2020-10-01 09:04:26). *Record keeping - WorkSafe ACT.* https://www.worksafe.act.gov.au/health-and-safety-portal/managing-safety/record-keeping

Worksafe (WA). (2023). *Interpretive Guideline Incident Notification.* Retrieved from https://www.wa.gov.au/system/files/2023-02/231149_GL_IncidentNotification.pdf

The Health and Safety Management System

The basic health and safety system

The process of establishing the core elements of a safety system can be traced through a series of common law proceedings. As already discussed elsewhere.

The basic safety system involves establishing, maintaining, promoting and propagating a safe system of work and this includes the deployment of competent staff and sufficient materials and equipment (*Wilsons & Clyde Coal Co v English*, 1938).

The statutory model of the WHS system is much more complex but has at its core Duties and roles, Safe systems of work that take into consideration Environment, egress and exit, Plant and equipment, Systems of work, Usage and handling, Facilities and amenities, Instruction, training and supervision, monitoring, consultation and the provision of resources such as PPE (*Model Work Health and Safety Act 2011*, Austl.).

Various business and industry standards such as the Occupational health and safety management systems - Requirements with guidance for use. (ISO 45001:2018) have

127

tried to capture the essence of a sound WHS management system (Standards Australia, 2018). The WHS system described in this book for the most part extends the information found in ISO 45001:2018.

A successful WHS system is a broad system with continual improvement. It includes practical evidence as well as administrative evidence that the safety of the workers and all those concerning the PCBU and its work function are safe. To achieve this, 3 broad areas must exist:

1. Instruction through planning, leadership, consultation, cooperation training and supervision.
2. Resources include provision, storage, maintenance encouragement, and participation of workers in the safety system.
3. Systems of work and operations which include, administrative support for the Instruction and Resources and this also includes change and risk management.

These three categories encompass the basic common law and statutory requirements for a successful WHS system. It would be naïve to think that having a complete system that does not minimise injury or disease is successful, or that a system lacking these qualities yet has no injuries or diseases is also successful. A successful system requires intent and purpose and from within that intent and purpose derive the fruits of the labour.

Organisational Context

One of the most difficult aspects of a health and safety management system to establish is the correct identification and treatment of the organisational context. Most people are inclined to ask or retrieve information from those within the formal structure. If this idea is followed, then each level of the organisation will have a series of inputs and ideas that shape the expectations and scope of the WHS system.

However, many organisations such as churches, social clubs and non-profits use a slightly different model. Often, they have external steering committees that can influence substantially the organisation and yet have no particular formal role within the organisation. This is considered in broad terms the impact of external stakeholders. External stakeholders can hold businesses and organisations at ransom if they are the primary source of monetary support. For instance, two projects may be considered but one needs to be chosen. The organisation's CEO and Directors agree with say project A. However, they receive verbal communication, that is undocumented, and from the informal Steering committee. The informal steering committee states that they will not give any funding or assistance for project A but will do so for project B. In this way and similar manners of ransom, many organisations are swayed. For the churches trying to hang onto their assets and pay their wages, it takes little imagination the impact of monetary support and its influence.

These external stakeholders and their impact require astute and clear assessment. There is nothing worse than trying to implement something that will not receive the resources or funding that is required. This is especially true and significant when the change required or the desired objective has to do with the health, safety and wellbeing of those involved.

The scope of the organisation is the well-defined policy that is being achieved. It may be more than the formal WHS policy and may include;

1. External stakeholder impact
2. Formal Policy for WHS
3. All products and services linked to WHS performance

As noted earlier the WHS management system must have in place not only compliance but continual improvement beyond compliance. Initially, many organisations struggle with full compliance and they will have some areas that are essentially non-compliant with legislation. When an inspector determines compliance, they do not have headroom to make subjective tests but rather focus on objective tests. This means that usually, something is either compliant or not. It can't be a measure or level of compliance that is reported. This is especially true for most machinery-based criteria and penalties related to them. Other areas are open to interpretation and may require legal counsel such as issues of due diligence and the duty of care. Underlying the level of compliance is the issue of what is considered reasonably practicable. Reasonably practicable means that at some point some risks need to be managed rather than eliminated. However, deciding which ones to manage and which ones to eliminate requires careful consideration.

There is an objective test for what is reasonably practicable. The test, as noted elsewhere, has the following elements:

1. Assessing the likelihood of the risk or hazard causing an effect on the objective of the WHS system.
2. The level of harm or detrimental impact from the hazard or risk.
3. Knowledge, information and consultative data are concerned with eliminating or minimising the risk or hazard.
4. The availability and suitability of ways to eliminate and manage the risk or hazard.
5. Costs to achieve the desired outcomes.

As a word of warning, costs although part of the objective test, will vary substantially between organisations. What will be cost-effective in one organisation will be different for another. The ability of an organisation to eliminate a risk or hazard based on cost has to be considered in conjunction with the other areas or points mentioned. Most notable are the likelihood and extent of impact. Also, it should be clear that when the test is conducted it takes into account only the legal entities, not the informal steering committees or other such external stakeholders. By this method of manipulation, the external stakeholders remain immune to the law and in contrast, those within the organisation are impacted by the legal process.

There are two significant types of organisational context. We now turn to the formal structure of organisations and their functions. The Entrepreneurial and Intrapreneurial. The entrepreneurial organisation focuses mainly on taking risks to take advantage of opportunities as they arise. The intrapreneurial organisation tends to evade taking risks but takes advantage of opportunities. The difference between the organisations is subtle. Organisational contexts that can also be used in conjunction with this umbrella category include Mature v Immature organisational context, Professional v Trade organisational context, Innovative v Standardised organisation etc. All these contextual views will affect how the organisation will develop its strategic process.

Organisational context from experience can be divided as follows:

1. **Entrepreneurial**
   Stylised by a centric form of governance that relies heavily on the involvement of the CEO and delegation is restricted.
2. **Mature Machine**
   Stylised by a well-established highly regulated, integrated and often bureaucratic management system.
3. **Professional**
   Stylised by being driven by professional input and contributions from separate entities that rely on administrative assistance to achieve standardised products and services.
4. **Innovative**
   Stylised by the formation of ad hoc teams made up of specialists that are necessary to drive the organisational agenda and at the same time innovate.
5. **Diversified**

> Stylised by the inclusion of several Mature Machine entities as semi-autonomous entities within its umbrella of integrated management. Most have departments or divisions with a headquarters or leading administrative group.
> (Mintzberg & Quinn, 1996).

Overall, several different approaches exist in determining what exact organisational context is being dealt with. If we look at the functional side of organisational context we derive to:

Postpositivist

Quantitatively driven and where quantification cannot occur, qualitative data is considered. Goals tend to align with external global agendas and frameworks (Linklater, 2007).

Pragmatic

Qualitative systems are used predominantly and most of the treated data is qualitative. Goals are qualitatively set and treated. Achievements towards specific, qualifiable, attainable, realistic and timely goals (Creswell & Creswell, 2017; Saunders et al., 2009).

Transactional

Legal and standard-based contracts or agreements drive the operation of the organisation. It tends to focus on goal achievement, rewards and penalties (Hudson, 2016).

Transformative

Usually, the organisation is driven by a larger-scoped agenda. The greater good or goal is so important that there is a focus on the steps needed to attain the ideal without much emphasis on penalties (Collins, 2018; Linklater, 2007).

Constructivist

These companies tend to have limited internal resources and knowledge and use it to learn pragmatically. So that through trial and error, there is a gradual improvement. These organisations tend to be reactive but not always and they tend to have directional goals instead of specific goals (Creswell & Creswell, 2017).

At any given point there may be a combination of these methods. This is why they can be somewhat difficult to identify and work with. If we look at the businesses by their structure it lends towards the leadership style being identified. Using the structural scope of the organisational context we obtain a clearer boundary but less to work with initially.

Autocratic

One person leads.

Oligarchical

A group or a few groups lead.

Pleistarchical

The workers lead themselves with few interruptions.

(modified from Aristotle, 2000).

We can see how the previously mentioned functions would operate differently within the various structures and contexts. For example, **Autocratic – Pragmatic** or **Autocratic – Transformative** etc. In this combined way we can get to understand the organisational context more thoroughly. Therefore, taking into account organisational context types, we could state **Oligarchical – Pragmatic - Diversified** would describe many large private organisations. Whereas an **Oligarchical – Transactional – Mature Machine** organisation would be representative of something like a government regulator.

Using the order **Structure – Functional Approach – Context type,** we can describe several different organisations but not necessarily always. For example, an **Autocratic – Postpositivist – Professional** organisation may also be an **Autocratic – Pragmatic – Professional** organisation. For example, a private hospital could fit into the previous two models. However, it can also be Oligarchical or Pleistarchical and any selection of approaches in leadership as well as functions and contexts will affect the model. But if we were to choose the best fit for a modern hospital with government involvement and part-privatisation in Australia, an **oligarchical – pragmatic – professional** organisational context would suit or fit best in most such hospitals.

Leadership and worker participation

Many contemporary writers will emphasise the importance of good leadership in WHS. A world that is open, transparent and works for the sake of following a higher ideal we often refer to as the pinnacle good can exist. However, as noted leadership can come from within and without the organisation. It is more than the formal structure that we are concerned with but rather the informal structure based on power and influence. Leadership is the ability to cause action in an individual or group that is desired by the leader or leaders.

Some leadership models identified by Patrick Hudson are the autocratic, transactional and transformational types. He describes the autocratic model as being based on a benevolent, charismatic individual with sway in the workplace. The transactional leadership model is based on the agreement between PCBU entities about what is safe and where safety needs to be and those that cause harm or impede the system are reprimanded. The transformative style of leadership is based on encouragement through emotive awareness and consultation of a change towards set targets. Often it places blame second or of less importance (Hudson, 2016). We can liken transactional and transformative to the old school vs the new school model. Transactional models are like a contract between parties and have penalties derived from a breach of that contract. Transformative tries to make everyone a winner by downplaying the penalties and slanting emphasis towards the positive reinforcement of successful goal attainment.

There is an alternative view perhaps less imaginative and more practical in terms of proving and measuring. There are three types of leadership, Autocratic, Oligarchical and Pleistarchical. Autocratic leadership involves the scenario of order and obey model. Oligarchical is similar to the Autocratic model only that it usually has several sources such as the various input from departments. The Oligarchical system derives its orders through consensus between a small number of authorities. Pleistarchical leadership is derived from the majority and in that instance, we often see a very different model. The order and obey model shifts towards more of the directional order and directional adherence or obeying of that directional order. This means that there is a consensus of what should be done and this is the order or command. The steps to achieve the outcome are not specified and the adherence to the command is voluntary rather than authoritative obedience. At any given time, all three may exist but usually one is more prominent than another.

When the error, fault, or detrimental outcome is blamed or part of the pleistarchical collective normally it doesn't get much emphasis hence reinforcing also a transformative style. When an autocratic order or oligarchical order leads to a detrimental outcome on objectives then often it is highlighted be it transformative or transactional. It just stands out more when one or a few people can be isolated. But when it's the workforce it is harder to pinpoint and often falls back on what is called in part organisational culture.

Some styles are not based on the type of leadership count but on the nature of the leadership. It was already suggested that there is a direct relationship between pleistarchical systems and transformative approaches often leading to a blameless approach. Which can circumvent the criteria of accountability and responsibility. This failure or unwanted outcome is one of many found in all approaches. Hudson highlights some other unwanted outcomes derived from;

• telling and yelling

- teaching and patronising

- participating and doing it all

- delegating and advocating

(Hersey et al., 1979; Hudson, 2016).

We can see with some imagination that all these categories have some truth in them and will have different characteristics when applied to the leadership models of choice. The models can be the Hudson models or those I have suggested based on the number leading.

Whichever model is chosen, propped or developed, responsibility and accountability are required to be documented. This is a legal requirement as it relates to the duty of care. It is a simple and measurable aspect when one person blunders a situation and can take the blame. However, as the numbers become larger the difficulty in isolating the problem also increases. So much so, that large populations or groups of workers can effectively prevent responsibility or accountability from being established. This is of course a retrospective view in that we presume an incident has happened and an answer to it causation, responsibility and accountability are required. In the process usually, leadership is identified and treatment of the situation follows.

According to relevant standards, several criteria such as policies, procedures, resources, worker protection and several other important aspects are considered a part of leadership. These can be broken down into functions of leadership that entail Environmental, Plant and equipment,

Systems, Usage and handling, Facilities and amenities, and monitoring. These along with already mentioned aspects constitute the leadership of the qualities of the duty of care and due diligence. Leading resource allocation, ensuring it is being used properly and competently, and validating that policies and procedures are all being done as required are examples of leadership derived from the requirements of due diligence.

Overall, the leadership of the organisation needs to have specific qualities similar to those required for qualifying due diligence;

1. The knowledge they have of the workplace and its risks and hazards,
2. Nature of the hazards and risks and their impact,
3. Resource allocation, maintenance, training etc,
4. Information from consultation,
5. Compliance.
6. Verification

This suggests that if an external stakeholder requests a change in the workplace, and qualifies as a director under the Corporations Act, they may also need to be aware of their responsibilities and accountability of the legal leadership criteria imposed by due diligence. This of course is not always the case because many informal structures cannot prove one way or another that a person was a director or person with substantial influence in a workplace.

We don't see external stakeholders held accountable for the actions they lead, and as such extreme caution is required by the acting directors or formally structured leadership and management. Three basic outcomes will influence whether a leader in an organisation will implement the ideas influenced by a leader outside of the organisation.

In terms of Benefits:

External Low Impact v Internal High Impact

External changes cause a low beneficial impact on the WHS system. Internal alternatives have a highly beneficial impact on the WHS system. In this case, if there is low benefit in an externally imposed criteria or objective, it may be worth considering the highly beneficial impact of an internal alternative.

External Equivalent Impact v Internal Equivalent Impact

These events require careful consideration as there is little evidence-based criteria to use in assessing the impact of either venture, be it internal or external in origin.

External High Impact v Internal Low Impact

The high beneficial impact on WHS coming from an external stakeholder is very rare and almost unlikely. However, if it were to occur it would take precedence over a low beneficial impact alternative.

We can also look at the other side of the coin using the extent of harm or unwanted impact on our objectives and that would look similar to the above except the decisions would be inverted that is that external low-risk impact v internal high-risk impact would suggest that we take the low-risk option stemming from external leadership.

From a regulator and national policy body perspective, that is a **mature machine – oligarchical - postpositivist** context, the following leadership goals are promoted

1. managing risks
2. clear roles and a strong team
3. good two-way communication
4. compliance with work procedures
5. learning and training
6. fairness, dignity and respect
7. supervisor support
8. a positive leadership and management style.

(Safe Work Australia, 2024c).

From the same context, we can list further qualities of a desired leader.

1. commit to safety
2. participates
3. encourage participation by others
4. integrates WHS part of the business
5. monitors and reviews performance
6. Commits resources to WHS improvement and change

(Hersey et al., 1979; Hudson, 2016; Safe Work Australia, 2024c).

Leadership responsibilities from a business perspective include;

1. Acting in good faith
2. Acting with due diligence
3. Acting honestly
4. Acting within the scope of employment
   (*Corporations Act 2001*, Austl.).

Leadership can be a very complex field of investigation and a leader can draw from military-styled leadership as much as from agrarian styles, trades, business, professional, spiritual or religious. Leadership is about getting some desired action from the subject. Agrarian skills of herding large numbers of people at canteens or ques etc. Strategic groups under military-styled leadership come into effect in task forces or tasked groups. Social relational strengths learned from religious leadership all play a significant role in culture (Daft, 2016). Together all these factors shape the style of leadership. Some are all-encompassing while others are leaning to one type or another.

Management and leadership differ substantially. Managers tend to work the system while the leaders tend to empower those around them. The empowerment comes from thoroughly investing in those around them from the workers to the visitors.

Table 28

Differences between managers and leaders

Managers	Leaders
Short term goals	Long term goals
Analytical and convergent	Intuitive and divergent
Work the system	Improve the system
Hold people accountable	Build responsibility
Focus on outcomes	Focus on process
Train	Educate
Promote compliance	Promote ownership
Direct by edict	Inspire by example
Mandate rules and policies	Set expectations

(National Safety Council, 1997)

None of this explains why Alexander the Great's men jumped the walls of Babylon to save him when he led the charge prematurely. Nor does any of this describe in completeness his leadership style. The same could be said of the likes of Napolean De Bonepart or Issac Washington and so forth. Leadership as defined here is what the international, national and state governance want from business leaders and managers. It does not necessarily equate to what makes a great leader.

Planning

Usually, an agenda is required to start with. The agenda takes into consideration matters that form the organisational context internally and externally. Internally things like policy, plans and procedures are considered for planning. Administrative structures are the basis of initial planning. While managers will focus on short-term goals, the leaders will be looking for long-term solutions. In all the agenda will be changed from time to time and as such the planning phase will go through a flux or roundtrip of continual improvement. Therefore, the initial agenda may look at formalising and recognising informal structures and functions.

The next stage of planning involves the overall assurance system. That is the system that assures the integrity and credibility of the criteria and objectives under consideration for planning. Usually, this involves authoritative and professional objectives. The purpose of the assurance is to assure that the WHS management system and all matters detailed in the duty of care, due diligence and required compliance-related materials are considered.

In AS45001:2018 they discuss risks and opportunities that can be used to minimise the impact of the risks and take advantage of the opportunities to improve WHS. These matters would also require consideration in the WHS planning phase. This includes considering hazard and risk identification and treatment processes. Assessment and treatment of opportunities (Standards Australia, 2018).

In addition, action planning should consider the previous and include things like emergency response, compliance, technical options, financial matters and business matters.

Finally, clear goals need to be planned out. One approach is to consider if the goals are Specific, measurable, achievable overall, realistic and can be achievable within a reasonable period. But this is only one type of goal that can be achieved.

Planning WHS systems means taking everything that affects WHS and formalising a plan to ensure the maintenance and improvement of that WHS. To do this compliance is usually sought after first and then continual improvement begins. Although it can be argued that continued improvement is used to attain compliance, as discussed, usually you are either compliant or not. Therefore, compliance usually is achieved by deliberate short-term actions that aim to improve the level of health and safety.

Continual improvement and WHS planning involve some integration:

Plan: Plan for objectives and resources, taking into account opportunities and risks.

Do: Implement what was planned

Check: Implementation check to compare with the plan

Act: Amend course to resolve items identified during the check process (Standards Australia, 2016).

Planning system

The planning phase of the WHS management system needs to consider the following broad areas:

1. organisational context
2. statistical model and performance indicators
3. management of objectives
4. leadership of objectives
5. support or auxiliary objectives and management
6. workforce participation and management
7. resource management
8. compliance management
9. risk management
10. quality management

As part of the scope of the planning, there has to be the desire to improve the organisations' WHS standards and quality. Otherwise, the organisational context requires addressing.

The statistical model and performance indicators develop over time as the system is established. The initial statistics and performance indicators would be things like a cost-benefit analysis to highlight the potential or fiscal benefits of the WHS management system.

Management objectives will be driven in several ways such as influences from external or internal sources. Internally there may be an apex to base drive or base to apex drive. Leaders may create movements that benefit the company especially when given clear directions. Leadership objectives may differ from formalised management objectives but may be included in the objectives set for management. An example would be the workplace's need to meet job function KPIs like the number of items produced or services rendered. The management objectives would be the achievement of the KPIs through resource allocation and overall risk and quality management. The leadership objectives would be to motivate the workforce to work smarter and perform better.

Workforce participation and management lead to many specialised areas such as contractor management, compliance management and human resource management. The process of managing the workforce becomes a duty for both managers and leaders. While the managers define the boundaries the leaders push the moral, drive and innovation.

Resource management similar to workforce management focuses on all areas, material and human. This will be addressed more thoroughly under the heading Support. For now, it is appropriate to recognise that the planning phase will need to consider the support and operational resources needed, including all the WHS resources.

Compliance management objectives would be at the core of the planning process. Not for the sake of compliance alone, but for the sake of reducing risks at the same time. All areas of WHS, machine guarding, occupational hygiene, chemicals, fire, dispute resolution, consultation, emergency etc need to be considered. This is the arm of management that looks at the legal framework, constituent legislation and cases inspiring change and compliance.

Risk management, in conjunction with compliance management, works towards minimising the risks in the workplace. Risks should be eliminated or treated using the hierarchy of risk management.

Quality management takes all of the previous matters and attempts to improve each function. It also affects the structural aspects of the system. Therefore, the quality management system is an integrated system for the WHS management system. The planning of quality-related improvement is vital towards ensuring things are current and that the assurance mentioned earlier is being addressed and verified.

AS45001:2018 uses two broad planning categories,

a.) Actions to address risks and opportunities and

b.) OH&S objectives and planning to achieve them.

Rather than relay the information directly, experience and knowledge are applied to the criteria mentioned in the Standard to produce a guide on how things can be alternatively planned.

We have already covered the general planning approach. Where the context, interested parties and scope of the management system play a role in determining how the plan will manifest. However, as discussed, there needs to be a willing participation of the organisation as a whole in improving WHS standards.

Risk and Opportunities

Hazard identification is expected to be proactive and ongoing. From a technical view, the organisation of work itself can be scrutinised. What is the workload? The average hours worked? Etc.

Caution should be given to routine and non-routine activities and anything that could be considered foreseeable. Taking into account material and human factors.

Historic or lag data may lead to finding opportunities to evade certain repeating incident types. They also help identify potential emergencies.

The people in the workplace should always be considered. Including their exits and egress to the workplace. Sometimes certain matters become identified as issues that require resolving systematically, as described elsewhere.

Changes in knowledge of information about hazards, risks workplace changes etc need to also be planned for.

In conjunction with the previous, there is a need for a formal process to analyse and assess the WHS risks in conjunction with industry standards. The process should always look at the opportunities as well as the risks so that the chance to better the system is taken at the correct time and place.

When all the hazard-related identification, analysis, assessment, monitoring, review and feedback systems are planned for there is a time to enact the changes. Two areas stand out in the Standard. The first is the actions that address risks and opportunities, legal requirements, compliance and emergencies. The second is how to integrate and implement actions into WHS and evaluate its effectiveness.

OHS Objectives and Planning

The WHS objectives shall

1. Be communicated
2. Follow consistently the WHS policy
3. Be measurable or capable of performance evaluation
4. Take into account risks and opportunities

5. Be done with consultation between managers, leaders and workers
6. The whole process requires monitoring and updating as needed (Standards Australia, 2018).

Support

Support or auxiliary service usually works with operational management to achieve the organisational objectives. Support systems address the due diligence of the officers and also the diligence expected from workers. It also establishes critical auxiliary structures and functions.

Resources

All material resources require correct maintenance and management. The term resource management may reflect the correct procurement, provision, maintenance, allocation, tagging, use and handling. Concerning human resources and administrative resources, these must also be considered to ensure sufficient people are involved, of the correct competency and with adequate training and or supervision to do the job or jobs safely.

Competence

While some overlap with other areas exists, competency is usually established through qualifications and experience. Therefore, the process of competency management involves those who have skills that can complement the statistical model used for performance indicators. For instance, one may have good language skills and the other not so strong language skills. It would be viable to place those with language skills in positions to allow them to complement consultation and cooperative communication. While the lesser abled in communication would be enabled to input and encouraged to input based on what they can express. This creates an inclusive workplace and tiers responsibilities and accountability in line with abilities.

Proving competency is usually a case of documenting training, supervision, education and all actions that attempt to develop the personnel needed for a given job.

Awareness

It is very important to start the process of awareness through an induction that highlights the OHS or WHS policy. From there specific groups are trained and educated in the procedures for the business. There is a tendency by the current WHS systems to require a level bar indicating the knowledge and experience needed for individuals to perform given tasks. In the construction industry an attempt to raise awareness involved the nationally recognised "construction induction card" which has the common name "White card" around the country.

The induction involves learning the core principles of WHS and its importance in the workplace.

In businesses where H&S representatives are present additional training is required to get their certification. Traditionally the H&S induction program is detailed and covers a lot of the information. In places without H&S

representatives, personnel were traditionally trained in H&S training material. So that all the personnel were equipped with the knowledge that a H&S representative would be expected to know. In contrast, a substantial number of big companies such as mining companies, tend to put all their job-specific safety matters into their induction training packages. Therefore, there is variation across industries and between businesses as to where the bar sits in terms of expected H&S awareness.

Once the induction is over, usually ongoing interaction with specific issues is needed in the form of prestart meetings. The scope of these meetings should be multi-dimensionally scoped towards keeping everyone safe and healthy. This includes all the topics discussed as a part of the WHS management system, from context to quality. This component is also a part of the communication systems.

Communication

There are several types of communication. The face-to-face relayed verbal, video and relayed written communication. Face-to-face communication involves the meeting and discussion of WHS issues between those present. Relayed, video and audio, usually involve radio talk communication. It is often used to keep in touch with isolated workers. Relayed written communication is usually used to convey emails, memos, messages and so forth between those involved. Usually, they carry information that is deemed better suited to the written format. Although relayed video entails an image as well as audio, the usual method of communication is relayed audio. People with hearing disabilities may communicate via video with those who understand the language.

Communication, internally and externally, impacts more than operations alone but all facets of the organisation (Standards Australia, 2018). From Organisational context through to quality management all areas of the WHS system will require interfaces where communication can occur. From personal devices through to regular meetings each part of the organisation requires a method to communicate and consult between relevant parties.

Overall, the support systems require careful documentation and record-keeping. As discussed under the statistical model the performance indicators may be minutes of meetings through to transcripts of conversations etc. Documentation control is necessary as stipulated as part of the quality management system.

Documented Information

Depending on the type of information, where and when it will be used considerations should be given towards how the information will be processed. This will entail systems for Acquisition, data entry, process, storage, retrieval, disposal, publication and communication.

Overall quality management systems support the concept of stringent document control. It is therefore important to ensure that the latest, most current and accurate information is processed. It goes beyond our purposes to focus on data and document control. However, two areas often need focus on; "Are we using the latest plan?" and secondly "Where, when and how do we get rid of the old documents?"

Operation

The general operations of a business will vary from place to place. Operational aspects of the WHS management system focus on the processes and procedures that stem from the WHS policy. This involves taking into account the establishment, maintenance, promotion and propagation of WHS procedures and processes. It also includes risk control for specific tasks, change management, procurement and disposal of resources and equipment.

Hierarchy of Hazard Control

Specific jobs such as crane handling, forklifts, scaffolding and some types of pressure vessel work require high-risk licenses. These licenses contribute a way of establishing the competency of an individual.

In addition, jobs like welding, plastic forming, woodworking, fitting and turning etc all have specific PPE, procedures and processes that may vary from place to place, industry to industry and business to business.

A very basic model for managing risks starts with systems to identify, assess, treat and review them. The identification process at a technical level can be by observation or through injury statistics. In terms of culture and human behaviour, risks and hazards may be identified through audits. Then at the governance levels, accurate evidence-based reports go a long way in advising action from the governance tier of an organisation.

Despite the uniqueness of each hazard and its management, there is a legal standard across Australia to implement a hierarchy of risk and hazard controls. So that when a hazard or risk is identified, profiled, analysed, assessed, treated and reviewed there has been a consideration of the hierarchy of controls that can be implemented.

1. **Elimination**
   Eliminate the risks and hazards.
2. **Substitution**
   Substitute the risks and hazards with a less hazardous or lower risk.
3. **Isolation**
   Isolate the risk or hazard from the people
4. **Engineer**
   Engineer a solution to lower the risk or potential hazard.
5. **Administer**
   Provide an administrative procedure to handle retained risks and hazards.
6. **Personal Protective Equipment (PPE)**
   Provide PPE to help reduce retained risks and hazards.

Figure 8. *The Legislated Hierarchy of Risk Controls*

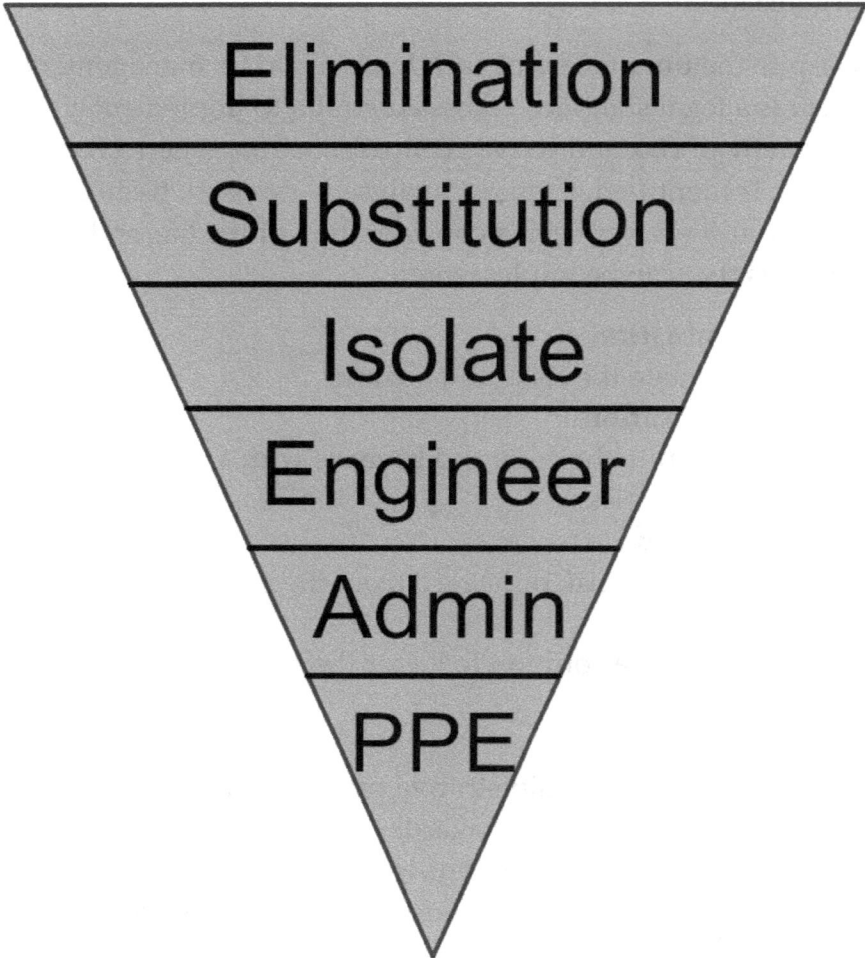

The shape of the inverted triangle denotes the priority of managerial focus and concern. The diagram indicates more focus and resources will be spent on eliminating risks and hazards than on providing personal protective equipment (PPE). Where previous legislation required PPE provision, the new model WHS laws require the implementation of this hierarchy in treating risks and hazards.

156

In some places, personnel are provided with a WHS manual to complement the operational aspects of WHS. This serves the purpose of informing workers, and anyone involved with the business, enough information to be aware of the risks and hazards on site.

Table 29

Case Study: Sanofi

Case Study: Sanofi - HSE Manual
Sanofi considers its company to be an innovative global healthcare company. The company is an Australian company that focuses on medicine and vaccines. In 2023 they published a WHS Manual that followed ISO 45001:2018. The organisational context was described as an innovative company that focused on governance standards from internal, external and international sources.

Note: The content of their HSE manual is not condoned.

Table 30

Case Study: Petrojet

Case Study: Petrojet – HSE Manual
Petrojet describes itself as a group among the biggest full-service construction groups in the Middle East and Africa Area. For a consistent period since 2022, their website has published with pride their Health and Safety manual. Their WHS manual also follows ISO 45001:2018 and expands the Operational component of the standard into various specific high-risk areas of operations. These include key safety concerns and procedures, vehicle safety, PPE, isolation, lock-out and use tags, confined spaces, emergency response, gas cylinder handling etc.

Note: The content of their HSE manual is not condoned.

Roles and responsibilities

As part of the operational concerns, there needs to be a clear and direct line of reporting, authority and responsibility. Roles and responsibilities need to be clearly defined. It should be noted that mines now have specific statutory roles and responsibilities for various classes of managers and supervisors. There are five statutory positions across the Australian States;

- site senior executive

- exploration manager

- underground manager (non-coal) if the mine is an underground non-coal mine

- underground manager (coal) if the mine is an underground coal mine

- quarry manager if required under the WHS Mines Regulations (Schedule 26, clause 14) (Department of Energy Mines Industry Regulation and Safety, 2022).

Because these are under review in several states at the time of writing, the nature of them is likely to change and won't be discussed in great detail. However, to be thorough each state has individual requirements that go beyond this basic set of statutory positions. For example, in Queensland, coal mining requires statutory positions for deputies, ventilation officers and several other positions (Business Queensland, 2015).

Tied to the roles and responsibilities is the matter of being fit for work. Usually, the fit for work is part of the contractor and workforce management process. Things that are considered are all aspects affecting the individual's ability to perform as expected.

1. Fatigue
2. Drugs and alcohol
3. Medical condition

Are the top three that make up the health standard? To determine the fit for work criteria. Pre-employment checks, periodic assessments and clear fitness standard development are required.

Health surveillance is required whenever there is the use of dangerous materials or chemicals and whenever there is reason to believe that the risks or hazards will have long-term effects. These may include relationships such as hearing and workplace noise exposure.

It should be noted that medical or mental health issues that have been treated and render the individual capable of work, should be considered and treated as if fit for work. People in this position should be treated with dignity and respect. People with some incapacity but otherwise are fit to work, should be treated like every other employee. Workplace provisions for any incapacity should be reasonably accommodated as necessary (World Health Organisation, 2024). As a signatory to the United Nations, the Australian States follow these guidelines.

Change Management

Operational aspects of the management system will need to take into account a substantial number of detailed and micro topics. In the process of developing the operational HS management system, there will be a need to change or modify the system.

WHS change management is concerned with all changes to the workplace. These can be temporary, emergency or permanent changes. In most organisations change is managed along a clear path between the desired change and the pragmatized change.

Figure 9. *Change management sequence*

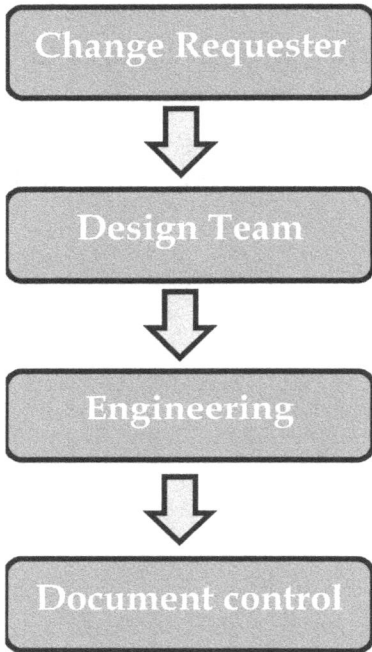

(Department of Energy Mines Industry Regulation and Safety, 2024)

The change requester can be apex-to-base or base-to-apex driven. The design team usually considers the change and its impact on the WHS of people in the workplace. Engineering looks at the residual risks and how they can be treated. Document control for the change should exist.

Another way of looking at change management is the transformative view.

1. Establish a need
2. Change designers
3. Create a vision
4. Communicate the vision
5. Empower others to act on establishing the vision
6. Plan short-term wins
7. Consolidating improvements and producing more change
8. Institutionalising new approaches and changes (Kotter, 1995).

In this model, the emphasis is on the collective power of the workforce working together in synergy with the vision. The consultative process takes a larger role than in other methods. While other methods exist, these are among the most popular in the industry at the time of writing.

Other more thorough and contemporary views on change management exist.

1. Fact gathering and problem definition
2. Assess and address the organization's readiness for change
3. Identify evidence-based change interventions
4. Develop change leadership throughout the Organization
5. Develop a compelling vision
6. Tap the influence of social networks
7. Promote micro-processes ("small wins") and experimentation (Rousseaua & Have, 2022).

Procurement

When change in the workplace involves purchasing or acquiring new resources. Certain criteria need to be considered. All introductions need to meet relevant Australian Standards and International Standards. For chemicals, it will be important to obtain Safety Data Sheets (SDS) before introducing the chemical to the workplace. Also ensuring that the supplier meets Australian Standards and International Standards is important. Knowing who you are dealing with in terms of designers, suppliers, and those demolishing or fitting structures. In particular, all States have similar legislation regarding the duties of those in control of fixtures, fittings and plant s.21, design plant, substances or structures s.22, import plant, substances or structures s24, supply plant, substances or structures s.25, install, construct or commission plant or structures s.26 (*Model Work Health and Safety Act 2011*, Austl., s.21-26). These requirements when procuring is legally binding and need immense caution.

In addition to these upstream matters, there are some financial matters related to WHS that also need to be addressed. In this section, we use the term "customer" to imply anyone in contract to provide, supply, design or procure any goods and services.

Specifications: All goods and services must be compliant with the required specifications.

Compliance and disclosure: There needs to be a disclosure of any matters that would affect the contract. Things like enforceable undertakings and general business law compliance are considered.

Capacity to Comply: A qualitative statement must exist to help determine if the engaged party is capable of fulfilling their WHS obligations.

Customer contract details: Any special conditions that could arise and that would elevate risks will require consideration and a plan to work around them or permit a contract cessation or deferment etc may apply.

Customer WHS systems: There must be proof of a WHS system in place especially if the customer intends to enter the workplace of the party engaging the customer (contractor). The WHS procedures must be submitted to the contractor. The Contractor then has to ensure that their activities do not alter the risks and plans of the customer and vis versa.

Training, reporting, and investigations: These three areas are negotiable and usually require shared resources. The contractor and customer have the onus to train, report risks and incidents, and investigate risks and incidents (Department of Finance, 2024).

Disposal

While the WHS laws cover upstream entities, it lacks comprehensive downstream coverage. The downstream coverage is encapsulated by duty to those affected by the work done, specifically the "Duties of other persons at the workplace.", s.29 (*Model Work Health and Safety Act 2011*, Austl.). Also, under common law, we have a relationship or neighbourly relation with those affected by the workplace even if they are not physically there, especially by our product or byproducts (*Donoghue v Stevenson*, 1932).

When procuring or engaging disposal services they need to follow the guidelines outlined under procurement. In addition, there are both federal and state laws regarding disposal and waste management.

Although each state has slightly different laws, they are more or less covering the same basic principles. One of the ongoing problems in Australia is the disposal of hazardous substances like Asbestos.

Table 31

Waste Management Laws by State

State	Waste Management Law
ACT	Waste Management and Resource Recovery Act 2016 Environment Protection Act 1997
NSW	Waste Avoidance and Resource Recovery Act 2001 Protection of the Environment Operations Act 1997
NT	Waste Management and Pollution Control Act 1998
Qld	Waste Reduction and Recycling Act 2011 Environmental Protection Act 1994
SA	Environment Protection Act 1993 Zero Waste SA Act 2004
Tas	Environmental Management and Pollution Control Act 1994 Waste and Resource Recovery Act 2020
Vic	Environment Protection Act 2017 Sustainability Victoria Act 2005
WA	Waste Avoidance and Resource Recovery Act 2007 Environmental Protection Act 1986
Federal	Recycling and Waste Reduction Act 2020

In general, there are three parties involved with waste disposal.

1. Waste producers;

2. Waste transporters; and

3. Waste receivers/treaters

(Worksafe (Vic), 2017).

Waste producers

Must perform risk assessments on the waste and determine how it will be segregated, handled, stored and transported.

Waste transporters

Must perform a risk assessment on the waste to determine if the waste is suitable for transport in its current state and remedy situations that can be done so safely. The driver must be aware of the SDS for the materials being transported and must have received adequate information to perform a risk assessment.

Waste receivers/treaters

The receivers are expected to sample the waste to determine if it has the same risk classification given by the producer and transporter. A relevant risk assessment is confirmed or established. Then the waste is processed according to Environmental Protection Authority guidelines.

Emergency Preparedness and Response

A template system for dealing with emergencies and their response is given under the chapter dealing with *Additional Components*. It is worth mentioning that specific plans are legally required to exist for emergencies. These emergencies may involve calling external help or dealing with things internally. Such as an Ambulance or a first aider. The planned response would consider the training, and testing of the system, evaluating its performance, communication systems needed, and factoring in the worker-by-worker risk profile. Some people will need a disabled ramp to get out. Please read the chapter heading *Emergency Procedures* under *Additional Components* for more information.

Performance evaluation

At some point, the Safety management system will need to justify, validate and account for its existence. More than this it will also need to ensure that the controls and processes can be verified. Common questions are is the workplace safer? Do we encounter fewer accidents? Can we improve what we are doing? Etc. To determine these things and similar questions we rely on performance indicators.

The statistical model used by a company, that is the data that the company collects, stores and processes will vary from industry to industry, company to company. The statistical model will contain more than performance indicators but also include an account for various aspects of the system. Therefore, accounting or proving that the duty of care has been compliant is an issue that can be determined with the correct information.

Using performance indicators from the statistical model can prove that certain levels of performance have been attained or are going to be attained if trends are maintained. At any given time, many performance indicators can be considered lead or lag indicators.

Performance management

The monitoring, measurement, analysis and performance evaluation begin with determining the organisational context. In the performance management model described here, an assumption is made that the organisation sits on a spectrum of maturity as described under Organisational Context. There are three spectral possibilities, immature, developing and maturing.

Immature: reactive, pathological. Resistant, becoming compliant.

Developing: informing, calculative, managing, developing awareness, working on improving beyond compliance

Maturing: proactive, generative, learning cooperating continuously improving (O'Neill & Wolfe, 2017).

Table 32

Common lead and lag indicators used in WHS management

Lead KPI	WHS Control	Lag KPI
Number of staff consulted	Consultation	Number of staff suggestions adopted
Percentage of machines guarded.	Guarding	Percentage of corrective actions being eliminated
Number of corrective actions completed	Hierarchy of controls	
	Risk Register	Number of machine-body incidents
Number of completed inspections	Inspection	Percentage reviewed based on schedule
Percentage of sites inspected		Number or percentage of non-conformances or improvements needed.

(adapted from O'Neill & Wolfe, 2017).

A significant amount of performance management is tiered in functions. Most safety professionals are focused on the fundamental performances of their tier and as such it is difficult to write comprehensively to encompass all tiers in all organisational contexts. Governance is usually associated with the apex tier of management. Cultural management is associated with middle to top-level management. Technical controls are usually left to supervisors and front-line managers.

We can define performance as:

Performance = Competence × Commitment × Culture + Opportunity factor leverage (modified from Venkateswara Rao, 2016).

Where competency addresses the question, did we get it right? Commitment addresses the requirements to allocate and commit resources. Culture is an extension of the people within the organisation. Opportunity refers to things that were taken advantage of in favour of a safer environment. This is ok for an individual but lacks some value for systemic applications.

We can alter the formula slightly for an organisationally independent system performance. WHS Performance (WHSP) can be estimated by the following: The top line maximum should equal 1 or 100 % and the bottom line should equal 1 or 100%.

$$\text{WHSP} = \frac{Comp. + Commit. + Gov. + Opportunity}{Period\ of\ time}$$

Note: *Comp. = Competence, Commit. = Commitment, Gov. = Governance.*

This abstract formula aligns more with the overall performance of a WHS management system. Competence takes the form of instruction, training, supervision etc. Commitment refers to the resources applied to achieve competency. Governance includes a measure of the system, its documentation and overall management and leadership.

The opportunities are the opportunities taken to improve the WHS system and align with the organisational context. The more opportunities the better the performance over a given time.

.

Monitoring, Measurement and Analysis

Monitoring and measuring systems will vary between organisations and the hazard involved. Some will monitor using surveillance systems, others with sensors and gauges, others will have a combination of many different monitoring systems. The unfortunate symptom of surveillance monitoring is that it is usually about as interesting as watching grass grow. It takes a special kind of person to diligently stare at a monitor for a whole shift. As for the traditional administrative monitoring systems, we have confined space monitoring and ongoing gas checks as well as fire monitoring after hot works to name a few. These tasks are tied to an administrative requirement to monitor the worker closely which is why it is often called sentry duty. These are some of the many technical-based monitoring and measurement methods. The type of monitoring and measurement relies heavily on what has been changed or the profile of the hazard control being monitored.

The next level is that of cultural-based monitoring and measurement. Depending on the culture the monitoring systems and measurements will vary. A postpositivist organisation that is developing maturity may consider monitoring and measuring changes in the workplace. They would give high regard in their analysis for achieving international standards and internal participation.

The higher level will consider overall governance and monitoring things like procurement contract fulfilment, reviews of changes, planning for the organisation and taking on board recommendations from within and without the system. Monitoring at the higher levels of management relies heavily on the contributions of reports and information that are accurate. Self-evaluation via management reviews is also common.

Some key areas that require focus are

1. Compliance
2. Hierarchy of control implementation and verification
3. Organisational objectives
4. Operational and other controls
5. Methods and procedures for monitoring, measuring and analysing performance
6. Establishing internal standards (Standards Australia, 2018)

Internal auditing

While the relevant standards have different headings to the one used here, the components of the system such as compliance management are part of the competency referred to in the performance evaluation process. Internal auditing is one of several mechanisms used to gain information. It is the preferred system in the industry at the moment. We will address it here to be thorough.

An audit is usually a review of performance indicators. There are three general areas of interest to the internal auditor. Firstly, the legal and standard compliance. Secondly the technical knowledge of the risks and hazards. Thirdly, the management and leadership practices that are desired (Moeller, 2016). For example, the provision of facilities may be a standard of industry and legality. The resources that need to be provided to procure and install the facility may be a management function. However, the actual functionality of those facilities is a technical issue. All three areas become internally audited taking into consideration the relevant statistical model and the performance indicators forming part of it.

Internal auditing forms an integrated tool that assists with monitoring, measuring and analysing performance indicators. Also, it is used in evaluating risks and opportunities. Furthermore, it is used in change management and the improvement cycle.

Improvement

Improvement in the workplace comes from looking at the risk profile of the business and the actions taken, determining the impact the system has on injuries, and the verification process through tools like audits (O'Neill & Wolfe, 2017).

For example, the flow of information should be constantly monitored especially timed events like the reporting obligations within set time frames. Given an incident that requires reporting to the regulator, the time frame of reporting the incident is considered a technical obligation. The same information would need to be turned into a report or part of a report, highlighting relevant injury performance indicators. Before reaching the apex, the verification officers in the organisation need to substantiate that what was intended to be done was actually done and that the system in place catered adequately for the injured party.

When information is treated in this way and with the scope of continually improving then the organisation is said to be developing maturity. However, as noted many styles of business exist and each one will look very different to the example given. The information given here is in line with the authoritative view of the regulator.

Incident, nonconformity and corrective actions

Incident management is a large area of study. When an incident or a nonconformity occurs, the organisation needs to take action. That action must be timely, effective in implementing and acting on the hierarchy of control and permit for a review of the consequential actions taken.

Continual Improvement

ISO 9001 has become the international standard for handling quality issues such as continuous improvement. The scope of continual improvement is that compliance is only the first step to be taken. Thereafter further improving the WHS standard should occur. This is done by taking into account better performance, promoting culture and support, promoting the participation of workers, and communication systems. Also, maintaining and retaining documentation and their version (Standards Australia, 2018).

The cycle of continual improvement has already been described, however a figure to represent the process is used to review the process.

Figure 10. *Continual Improvement and its relationship to established standards*

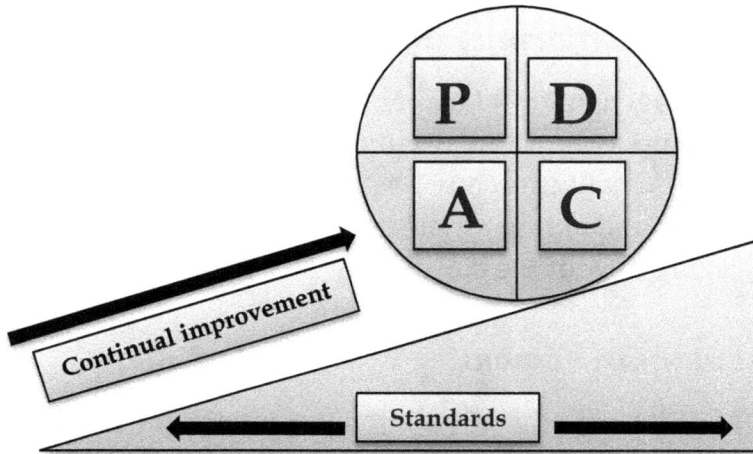

P = Plan, D = Do, C = Check, A = Adjust (modified from Standards Australia, 2016)

What happens during the PDCA Cycle?

The P Phase

The planning phase takes into account the matters raised under planning in the WHS system.

The D Phase

During the doing phase Support and Operation matters are handled.

The C Phase

The checking phase involves going through the performance criteria for each control in place.

The A Phase

The Adjust phase considers continual improvement as discussed under the heading Improvement.

Further Reading

Aristotle. (2000). Politics (B. Jowett, Trans.). In: Infomotions, Inc.

Business Queensland. (2015, 2015-02-26). *Coal mining competencies.* Queensland Government. https://www.business.qld.gov.au/industries/mining-energy-water/resources/safety-health/mining/competencies-certificates/coal

Collins, H. (2018). *Creative Research : The Theory and Practice of Research for the Creative Industries* (Vol. Second edition). Bloomsbury Visual Arts.

Corporations Act 2001. (Austl.). Retrieved from https://www.legislation.gov.au/Details/C2022C00306

Creswell, J. W., & Creswell, J. D. (2017). *Research Design* (5th ed.). SAGE Publications, Inc. (US).

Daft, R. L. (2016). *The Leadership Experience.* Cengage Learning.

Department of Energy Mines Industry Regulation and Safety. (2022, 2022-11-15). *What are statutory positions and who is eligible for appointment?* Western Australian Government. https://www.commerce.wa.gov.au/worksafe/what-are-statutory-positions-and-who-eligible-appointment

Department of Energy Mines Industry Regulation and Safety. (2024). *Management of change: guide.* Department of Energy Mines Industry Regulation and Safety. https://www.commerce.wa.gov.au/sites/default/files/atoms/files/241263_gl_managementofchange.pdf

Department of Finance. (2024). *Work Health and Safety in Procurement Guideline: Introductory guidance and model clauses.* https://www.wa.gov.au/system/files/2024-07/work-health-and-safety-in-procurement-guideline-july-2024.pdf

Donoghue v Stevenson [1932] UKHL 100. https://www.bailii.org/

Hersey, P., Blanchard, K. H., & Natemeyer, W. E. (1979). Situational leadership, perception, and the impact of power. *Group & Organization Studies (Pre-1986),* 4(4), 418. https://www.proquest.com/scholarly-journals/situational-leadership-perception-impact-power/docview/232429433/se-2

Hudson, P. (2016). *Safety Culture and Leadership*. Delft University of Technology.

Kotter, J. p. (1995, march/April). *Leading change: Why transformation efforts fail?* Harvard Business Review.

Linklater, A. (2007). *Critical theory and world politics : citizenship, sovereignty and humanity.* Routledge. http://site.ebrary.com/id/10204865

Mintzberg, H., & Quinn, J. B. (1996). *The strategy process: concepts, contexts and cases* (3rd ed.).

Model Work Health and Safety Act 2011. (Austl.).

Moeller, R. R. (2016). *Brink's Modern Internal Auditing: A common body of knowledge.* Wiley.

National Safety Council. (1997). *Supervisors' Safety Manual* (9th ed.). National Safety Council.

O'Neill, S., & Wolfe, K. (2017). *Measuring and reporting on work health and safety.* Safe Work Australia. https://www.safeworkaustralia.gov.au/system/files/doc uments/1802/measuring-and-reporting-on-work-health-and-safety.pdf

Rousseaua, D. M., & Have, S. t. (2022). Evidence-based change management. *Organizational Dynamics, 51*(3). https://doi.org/https://doi.org/10.1016/j.orgdyn.2022.10 0899

Safe Work Australia. (2024c). *Leadership and culture.* https://www.safeworkaustralia.gov.au/safety-topic/managing-health-and-safety/leadership-and-culture

Saunders, M. N., Lewis, P., & Thornhill, A. (2009). *Research Methods for Business Students* (5th ed.). Pearson Education.

Standards Australia. (2016). *Quality management systems – Requirements with guidance for use. (AS/NZS ISO 9001:2016).* . Retrieved from http://standards.org.au

Standards Australia. (2018). *Occupational health and safety management systems - Requirements with guidance for use. (ISO 45001:2018).* Retrieved from http://standards.org.au

Venkateswara Rao, T. (2016). *Performance management : towards organizational excellence* (2nd ed.). SAGE Publications India Pvt Ltd.

Wilsons & Clyde Coal Co v English [1938] AC 57.
https://www.bailii.org/

Worksafe (Vic). (2017). *Safe handling of industrial waste*. Worksafe (Vic) Retrieved from https://content-v2.api.worksafe.vic.gov.au/sites/default/files/2018-06/ISBN-Safe-handling-of-industrial-waste-guide-2013-05.pdf

World Health Organisation. (2024). *Mental health at work*. United Nations. https://www.who.int/news-room/fact-sheets/detail/mental-health-at-work

Additional Components

In this chapter, we briefly highlight some of the other requirements for the WHS management system in the Australian States.

Risk management is required to be integrated into the WHS system but there is no requirement for a stand-alone risk management department, division or system overall. The integrated function of the risk management system is done in a manner to minimises and treats risks using a hierarchy of controls.

Quality management systems can in some instances be compulsory in terms of regulating specific products. Compliances with strict standards for medicine and related products mean that a quality system is required.

"Quality Management System (QMS) for the design, production, packaging, labelling and final inspection of a device, and inspection and quality assurance techniques that are to be applied during the production of a device..." (Therapeutic Goods Administration (TGA), 2019).

In almost every other business model the requirement for a Quality management system is not specifically required. However, having said this many business types require some type of regulation from product-related issues such as seat belt functionality through to external interfaces such as environmental pollution.

Similarly, Health and Safety Committees and Representatives can enhance the business but are optional parts of the business model. When or if they exist means that specific aspects regarding keeping them informed, trained and part of the decision-making process are added to what is presented here in this book.

Consultation systems

General business consultation between the business operators and workers should exist to:

1. Provide and attain relevant safety information

2. raise WHS matters and issues

3. Consultative input on

    o   hazards and risks identification and processing

    o   Discuss and make decisions using the hierarchy of controls

    o   decisions regarding the adequacy of facilities

    o   proposed workplace changes that may affect safety and health

    o   decide and agree on health and safety procedures.

(Worksafe (Qld), 2020).

A consultation will need to take into account several other legislative requirements. There are currently 13 clauses that reference the need to consult. These requirements cover specific communication between the business operator (PCBU) and designers, suppliers, installers etc. A good reference is Appendix E and other parts of the *Code of Practice: Work Health and Safety Consultation, Cooperation and Coordination (2023)* (Safe Work Australia, 2023c).

Dispute Resolution

The minimum requirements for issue or dispute resolution are

1. **Issue Identification:** A WHS issue has been identified formally or informally. The party identifying the hazard must report it. Information to be relayed in the reporting is that an issue requires resolution and the scope of the issue.
2. **Consultation:** A meeting or formal communication is required between the parties. Throughout the entire process, regard must be given to the urgency and risks associated with the identified issue.
3. **Prioritisation:** As a minimum,
   a. The immediacy of risk to workers or other persons;
   b. the number and location of persons affected by the issue;
   c. the temporary and permanent controls and measures that must be implemented to resolve the issue;

      d. choosing those responsible for implementing the resolution measures

4. **Resolution Agreement:** If the issue is considered resolved a written agreement between involved parties must exist.

      a. All parties must be satisfied and have agreed to the resolution

      b. A copy must be given to all parties involved including any H&S Committees.

      c. At any time, the process can be re-started by raising matters with a H&S representative or independently.

Figure 11. *The basic issue-resolution process*

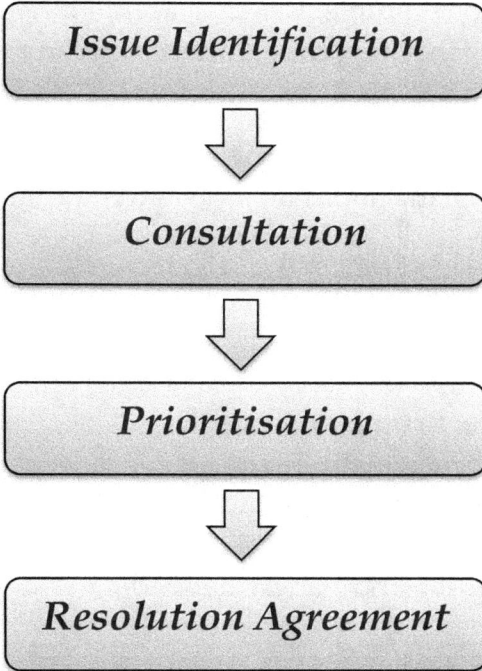

```
┌─────────────────────────────┐
│     Issue Identification     │
└─────────────────────────────┘
                ⬇
┌─────────────────────────────┐
│        Consultation          │
└─────────────────────────────┘
                ⬇
┌─────────────────────────────┐
│       Prioritisation         │
└─────────────────────────────┘
                ⬇
┌─────────────────────────────┐
│     Resolution Agreement     │
└─────────────────────────────┘
```

(*Model Work Health and Safety Regulations 2011*, Austl., r.23;
Work Health and Safety (General) Regulations 2022, W.A.)

Emergency Procedures

Emergency procedures will include incident responses as part of the process. For example, when an accident happens that triggers an emergency response, there is also an incident investigation required.

All Australian States require under their WHS Acts an emergency plan. The plan should include as a minimum:

1. **The scope of its application**
    What emergencies are likely to occur?
2. **Emergency Contacts**
    Who to contact for each type of emergency, police, fire, ambulance, first aid officer etc?
3. **Emergency Management Team**
    Who will respond to a raised emergency?
4. **Supervisors**
    The duties of front-line leaders defined
5. **Workers**
    Duties of workers defined.
6. **Evacuation procedures**
    What will happen in the process of evacuation?
7. **Post Emergency Actions**
    How to call off the emergency, what process to follow after the emergency etc.
8. **Testing the emergency plan**
    Fire alarm and evacuation drills.
9. **Training**
    Specific training related to the execution of the plan, such as training to deal with code black (personal threat) events.
10. **Reviewing and reporting**

Once the emergency is over the outcome should be reviewed. Did we leave anyone behind? Was it performed well and with minimal risks introduced? Also, the reports would include an incident or accident investigation.

11. **Record keeping and Document control**

The whole process requires documentation of the emergency response and its compliance with the plan being used. Also, documents must be controlled so that the correct procedures are in place (Safe Work Australia, 2012).

Sustainability

Sustainability and the United Nations go hand in hand with a global agenda to sustain a global culture of inclusiveness and cooperation. The published sustainability development goals include;

1. No Poverty
2. Zero Hunger
3. Good health and wellbeing
4. Quality education
5. Gender equality
6. Clean water and sanitation
7. Affordable and clean energy
8. Decent work and economic growth
9. Industry innovation and infrastructure
10. Reduced inequalities
11. Sustainable cities and communities
12. Responsible consumption and production

13. Climate action
14. Life below water
15. Life on land
16. Peace, justice and strong institutions
17. Partnerships for the goals.

(United Nations - Department of Economic and Social Affairs)

You may then ask the question what has this to do with WHS? WHS comes under several goals such as SDG-3 Good health and well-being. Of course, in some communities, SDG-1 poverty, and SDG-2 hunger, also play a role in how WHS is implemented. For example, undernourished workers and deciding who bears the PPE costs etc will impact how WHS can be addressed.

Other SDGs that impact WHS are as follows:

SDG 3: Good Health and Well-being – For example, the proper handling and disposal of waste, helps prevent incidents and promotes overall health.

SDG 6: Clean Water and Sanitation - Implementing safety protocols in water treatment and distribution systems ensures access to safe and clean drinking water.

SDG 7: Affordable and Clean Energy - Safety measures in the energy sector, including the safe handling of renewable energy technologies. Electrical safety and its implementation in renewable energy models is a new and innovative frontier. The other scope of WHS in this SDG is to contribute to the reliable and sustainable supply of clean energy.

SDG 8: Decent work and economic growth

SDG8.7 Calls for the eradication of modern day slavery. Areas given priority in concern are:

1. Supply Chains,
2. Migration,
3. Rule of Law and Governance,
4. Conflicts and Humanitarian Settings.

SDG 9: Industry, Innovation, and Infrastructure - Adopting International Safety Standards in industrial processes and infrastructure development helps build resilient and sustainable industries. The benefit of WHS to achieving the SDG is important. Industry and infrastructure are changing the landscape and along with it, WHS needs to adapt to the infrastructure and industry innovations.

SDG 11: Sustainable Cities and Communities - Ensuring the safety of buildings and public spaces through rigorous safety standards and regulations supports the development of sustainable and resilient cities. From a *people* perspective, sustainable cities and communities require attention to how well people can live in them.

SDG 13: Climate Action – As discussed as part of the disposal of resources, the WHS team has an Environmental sustainability goal. That goal is to ensure that the environment receives minimal impact and that the processes align with international and state regulations.

In addition to the above the United Nations and its involvement with Human Rights have been in progress around the world for decades. In 2011 the UN published the

Guiding Principles on Business and Human Rights. This also ties WHS with the human right to enter and leave work without remarkable risks to safety and health (United Nations, 2011).

Sustainability in WHS practice can take on many forms. Technically, the work health and safety issues will focus on the new and innovative changes being made in our world. The managerial, leadership and governance of these issues will take on a tripartite view of International, State and Industry standards.

Further Reading

Model Work Health and Safety Regulations 2011. (Austl.).

Safe Work Australia. (2012). *Emergency plans fact sheet.* https://www.safeworkaustralia.gov.au/system/files/doc uments/1702/emergency_plans_fact_sheet.pdf

Safe Work Australia. (2023c). *Model Code of Practice - Work health and safety consultation, cooperation and coordination.* (978-0-642-33299-8 (PDF)). Retrieved from https://www.safeworkaustralia.gov.au/sites/default/file s/2023-08/model%20Code%20of%20Practice%20-%20WHS%20consultation%2C%20cooperation%20and%20 coordination%20-%20July%202023_2.pdf

Therapeutic Goods Administration (TGA). (2019, 2024-10-03T15:23+10:00). *Guidance on Therapeutic Goods (Conformity Assessment Standard for Quality Management Systems) Order 2019.* https://www.tga.gov.au/guidance-therapeutic-goods-conformity-assessment-standard-quality-management-systems-order-2019

United Nations - Department of Economic and Social Affairs. *The 17 Goals.* United Nations - Department of Economic and Social Affairs. https://sdgs.un.org/goals

United Nations. (2011). *Guiding Principles On Business and Human Rights.* United Nations. https://www.ohchr.org/sites/default/files/Documents/ Publications/GuidingPrinciplesBusinessHR_EN.pdf

Work Health and Safety (General) Regulations 2022. (W.A.).

Worksafe (Qld). (2020). Consultation, representation and participation. Retrieved 2020-06-26 12:00:09, from https://www.worksafe.qld.gov.au/laws-and-compliance/work-health-and-safety-laws/consultation-representation-and-participation

Additional Components

End Notes

Introducing Work Health and Safety in the Australian States takes a new and refreshing view of Australia and its States. Each one with unique demographics and issues relating to Work Health and Safety. Writing this book was very enjoyable and, in some ways, frustrating as the aim was to keep it under 250 pages. It is my first attempt to fulfil ISO 45001 requirements and the legal requirements in one volume, concisely. Although concise, I believe it is detailed enough to be considered of value to the WHS professional. I truly hope you get a lot out of this publication.

This book is only a guide. Each heading and subheading are massive areas of investigation and constitute many books of information. Your feedback on the book will assist in the betterment of future versions. Also, a special thank you to all those who supported me professionally.

About The Author

Tim Damianidis is a dynamic multifaceted individual who has worked in businesses at all levels from worker to director and almost everything in between. He has many years of experience working in work, health and safety and general business management. Also, he has postgraduate qualifications in Work Health and Safety.

Complete References

Adar, Y. (2012). *Comparative Negligence and Mitigation of Damages: Two Doctrines in Search of Reunion.* https://papers.ssrn.com/sol3/papers.cfm?abstract_id=2078874

Adelaide Law Review. (1963). Negligence: Novus actus interveniens - rescuer killed by negligence of third party - apportionment of liability - contributory negligence of rescuer. *The Adelaide Law Review, 10*(2), 112.

Agricola, G. (1556). *De Re Metallica* (H. C. Hoover & L. H. Hoover, Trans.). The Mining Magazine.

Alberta Labour and Immigration. (2020). *Reforming the Occupational Health and Safety (OHS) Legislation in Alberta - Discussion Guide.* Alberta Labour and Immigration.

Aristotle. (2000). Politics (B. Jowett, Trans.). In: Infomotions, Inc.

Australia. (2008). *Inter-Governmental Agreement for Regulatory and Operational Reform in Occupational Health and Safety* Federation of Australia. https://federation.gov.au/

Australia. (2009). *Occupational health and safety harmonisation.* Department of Employment and Workplace Relations,. https://www.dewr.gov.au/

Australian Bureau Of Statistics. (2023). *Work-related injuries.* Australian Bureau Of Statistics. https://www.abs.gov.au/

Australian Bureau of Statistics. (2024). *Counts of Australian Businesses, including Entries and Exits.* https://www.abs.gov.au/statistics/economy/business-indicators/counts-australian-businesses-including-entries-and-exits/latest-release.

Australian Capital Territory. (2024). *ACT Courts.* https://www.courts.act.gov.au/

Bolt, J., & Zanden, J. L. v. (2024). *Gross domestic product (GDP) 1820 - 2022*. Our World In Data. https://ourworldindata.org/

Business Queensland. (2015, 2015-02-26). *Coal mining competencies*. Queensland Government. https://www.business.qld.gov.au/industries/mining-energy-water/resources/safety-health/mining/competencies-certificates/coal

Caparo Industries plc v Dickman [1990] 2 AC 605.

CCH. (1991). *Planning Occupational Safety and Health* (3rd ed.). CCH.

CCH. (2024a). *Australian Workers Compensation Commentary*. CCH IntelliConnect.

CCH. (2024b). *Obligations around termination of employment (notice and keeping job open)*. http://intelliconnect.ezproxy.ecu.edu.au/scion/secure/ctx_10654914/index.jsp?cpid=WKAP-TAL-IC#page[3]

Clark, M., Eaton, M., Lind, W., Pye, E., & Bateman, L. (2011). *Key Statistics - Small Business Publication*. Commonwealth of Australia. https://treasury.gov.au/sites/default/files/2019-03/SmallBusinessPublication.pdf

Coady, D. A. (2002). Testing for Causation in Tort Law. *Australian Journal of Legal Philosophy*, 3(27), 83. https://classic.austlii.edu.au/au/journals/AUJlLegPhil/2002/3.pdf

Collins, H. (2018). *Creative Research : The Theory and Practice of Research for the Creative Industries* (Vol. Second edition). Bloomsbury Visual Arts.

Comcare. (2024). *Guidance for officers in exercising due diligence*. Comcare.

Connelly v RTZ Corporation Plc and Others [1997] UKHL 30. http://www.bailii.org/uk/cases/UKHL/1997/30.html

Corporations Act 2001. (Austl.). Retrieved from https://www.legislation.gov.au/Details/C2022C00306

Courts Administration Authority of South Australia. (2024). *Our Courts*. South Australia. https://www.courts.sa.gov.au/our-courts/

Creswell, J. W., & Creswell, J. D. (2017). *Research Design* (5th ed.). SAGE Publications, Inc. (US).

Daft, R. L. (2016). *The Leadership Experience*. Cengage Learning.

Department of Energy Mines Industry Regulation and Safety. (2022, 2022-11-15). *What are statutory positions and who is eligible for appointment?* Western Australian Government. https://www.commerce.wa.gov.au/worksafe/what-are-statutory-positions-and-who-eligible-appointment

Department of Energy Mines Industry Regulation and Safety. (2024). *Management of change: guide*. Department of Energy Mines Industry Regulation and Safety. https://www.commerce.wa.gov.au/sites/default/files/at oms/files/241263_gl_managementofchange.pdf

Department of Finance. (2024). *Work Health and Safety in Procurement Guideline: Introductory guidance and model clauses.* https://www.wa.gov.au/system/files/2024-07/work-health-and-safety-in-procurement-guideline-july-2024.pdf

Derrington, J. (1991). Proximity, the Standard of Care and Damage - Relating the Elements of Negligence. *University of Queensland Law Journal, 16*(2), 272.

Donoghue v Stevenson [1932] UKHL 100. https://www.bailii.org/

Grant v Australian Knitting Mills [1936] SASR 113. https://www.austlii.edu.au/

Grantham, D. (1992). *Occupational health and hygiene guidebook for the whso*. D.L. Grantham.

Greasley, D., & Oxley, L. (1998). A tale of two dominions: comparing macroeconomic records of Australia and Canada since 1870. *Economic History Review, 2*, 294. https://people.stfx.ca/

Hamilton v Nuroof (WA) Pty Ltd [1956] HCA 42.

Hammurabi. (1792 BC). *Code of Hammurabi* (R. F. Harper, Trans.). The University of Chicago Press.

Harrison, J. (2012a). Australian House of Representatives.

Harrison, J. (2012b). Australian Senate.

The Health and Social Care Act 2008 (Regulated Activities) Regulations 2014. (UK). Retrieved from https://www.legislation.gov.uk/uksi/2014/2936/regulati on/19/made

Herodotus. (450BC). *Histories*. TUFTS University. https://www.perseus.tufts.edu/

Herodotus. (1920). *Histories* (A. D. Godley, Trans.). TUFTS University. https://www.perseus.tufts.edu/

Hersey, P., Blanchard, K. H., & Natemeyer, W. E. (1979). Situational leadership, perception, and the impact of power. *Group & Organization Studies (Pre-1986)*, 4(4), 418. https://www.proquest.com/scholarly-journals/situational-leadership-perception-impact-power/docview/232429433/se-2

Hudson, P. (2016). *Safety Culture and Leadership*. Delft University of Technology.

Interpretive Guideline – Model Work Health And Safety Act The Meaning Of 'Reasonably Practicable'. (Austl.).

Jones, T. (2001). The Commonwealth v W L McLean: Developments Inconsistent with the Traditional Nature of the Egg Shell Skull Principle. *James Cook University Law Review*(8), 78.

Kotter, J. p. (1995, march/April). *Leading change: Why transformation efforts fail?* Harvard Business Review.

Labour Hire Licensing Act 2018. (Vic.). Retrieved from https://www.legislation.vic.gov.au/

Latimer v AEC Ltd [1953] UKHL 3. http://www.bailii.org/uk/cases/UKHL/1953/3.html

Linklater, A. (2007). *Critical theory and world politics : citizenship, sovereignty and humanity*. Routledge. http://site.ebrary.com/id/10204865

Mintzberg, H., & Quinn, J. B. (1996). *The strategy process: concepts, contexts and cases* (3rd ed.).

Model Work Health and Safety Act 2011. (Austl.).

Model Work Health and Safety Bill 2022. (Austl.).

Model Work Health and Safety Regulations 2011. (Austl.).

Moeller, R. R. (2016). *Brink's Modern Internal Auditing: A common body of knowledge*. Wiley.

National Safety Council. (1997). *Supervisors' Safety Manual* (9th ed.). National Safety Council.

New South Wales. (2024). *Communities and Justice*. https://courts.nsw.gov.au/

Northern Territory. (2024a). *Making a law in the Northern Territory.* Parliamentary Education Services. https://parliament.nt.gov.au/

Northern Territory. (2024b). *Types of courts and their roles.* https://nt.gov.au/law/courts-and-tribunals/types-of-courts-and-their-roles

O'Neill, S., & Wolfe, K. (2017). *Measuring and reporting on work health and safety.* Safe Work Australia. https://www.safeworkaustralia.gov.au/system/files/documents/1802/measuring-and-reporting-on-work-health-and-safety.pdf

Occupational Health and Safety Act 2004. (Vic.).

Owen, D. G. (2007). The Five Elements of Negligence. *Hofstra Law Review, 35*(4), 1671.

Paracelsus. (1541). *Four treatises of Theophrastus von Hohenheim* (C. L. Temkin, G. Rosen, G. Zilboorg, & H. E. Sigerist, Trans.). Johns Hopkins Press. https://archive.org/

Paris v Stepney BC [1951] AC 367. https://www.bailii.org/uk/cases/UKHL/1950/3.html

Parliamentary Education Office. (2024). *The responsibilities of the three levels of government.* Federation of Australia. https://peo.gov.au/

Queensland. (2024a). *Courts.* Queensland. https://www.courts.qld.gov.au/courts

Queensland. (2024b). *The Legislative Process - The Making of a Law (simplified).* Queensland Parliament. https://documents.parliament.qld.gov.au/

Queensland. (2024c). *Road and rail laws for dangerous goods.* Queensland. https://www.business.qld.gov.au

Ramazzini, B. (1700). *De Morbis Artificum Diatriba.* Typis A. Capponi. https://archive.org/

Reiff, N. (2023). *Leading Indicators: Definition and How They're Used by Investors.* https://www.investopedia.com/

Road Transport Reform (Dangerous Goods) ACT 1995 No. 34. (2024). Retrieved from http://www.austlii.edu.au/

Robens, L. A. (1972). *Safety and health at work - report of the Committee, 1970-72.* In *Committee on Safety and Health at Work* H.M.S.O. https://archive.org/

Rousseaua, D. M., & Have, S. t. (2022). Evidence-based change management. *Organizational Dynamics, 51*(3). https://doi.org/https://doi.org/10.1016/j.orgdyn.2022.100899

Safe Work Australia. (2012). *Emergency plans fact sheet.* https://www.safeworkaustralia.gov.au/system/files/documents/1702/emergency_plans_fact_sheet.pdf

Safe Work Australia. (2015). *Incident notification fact sheet - Incident-notification-fact-sheet-2015 UD.PDF.* https://www.safeworkaustralia.gov.au/sites/default/files/2022-09/Incident-notification-fact-sheet-2015%20UD.PDF

Safe Work Australia. (2020). *Template and example COVID-19 risk register.* https://covid19.swa.gov.au/doc/template-and-example-covid-19-risk-register

Safe Work Australia. (2023a). *Australia and other standards.* Safe Work Australia.

Safe Work Australia. (2023b). *Comparison of workers compensation arrangements in Australia and New Zealand 29th Edition (2023).* Safe Work Australia. https://www.safeworkaustralia.gov.au/sites/default/files/2024-04/comparison_of_workers_compensation_arrangements_in_australia_and_new_zealand_29th_edition_2023.pdf

Safe Work Australia. (2023c). *Model Code of Practice - Work health and safety consultation, cooperation and coordination.* (978-0-642-33299-8 (PDF)). Retrieved from https://www.safeworkaustralia.gov.au/sites/default/files/2023-08/model%20Code%20of%20Practice%20-%20WHS%20consultation%2C%20cooperation%20and%20coordination%20-%20July%202023_2.pdf

Safe Work Australia. (2024a). *Codes of Practice.* Safe Work Australia,. https://www.safeworkaustralia.gov.au/law-and-regulation/codes-practice

Safe Work Australia. (2024b). *Key Work Health and Safety Statistics Australia 2024.* Safe Work Australia.

Safe Work Australia. (2024c). *Leadership and culture.* https://www.safeworkaustralia.gov.au/safety-topic/managing-health-and-safety/leadership-and-culture

Safe Work Australia. (2024d). *Table 5.6: Common law provisions | Safe Work Australia.* Safe Work Australia. https://www.safeworkaustralia.gov.au/book/compariso n-workers-compensation-arrangements-australia-and-new-zealand-2021-28th-edition/chapter-5-benefits/table-56-common-law-provisions

SafeWork (NSW). (2024). *Legislation.* New South Wales. https://www.safework.nsw.gov.au/

SafeWork (SA). (2020, 2020-11-10). *Keeping records | SafeWork SA.* SafeWork (S.A.). https://www.safework.sa.gov.au/resources/simple-steps-to-safety/keeping-records

SafeWork (SA). (2024). *Legislation.* https://www.safework.sa.gov.au/

Saunders, M. N., Lewis, P., & Thornhill, A. (2009). *Research Methods for Business Students* (5th ed.). Pearson Education.

Smith v Charles Baker & Sons [1891] UKHL 2. https://www.bailii.org/uk/cases/UKHL/1891/2.html

Standards Australia. (1990). *Workplace injury and disease recording standard (AS 1885.1 1990).*

Standards Australia. (2016). *Quality management systems – Requirements with guidance for use. (AS/NZS ISO 9001:2016).* . Retrieved from http://standards.org.au

Standards Australia. (2018). *Occupational health and safety management systems - Requirements with guidance for use. (ISO 45001:2018).* Retrieved from http://standards.org.au

Stone v Bolton [1951] AC 850.

Tasmania, J. D. o. (2024). *Courts and Tribunals Tasmania.* https://www.courts.tas.gov.au/

Therapeutic Goods Administration (TGA). (2019, 2024-10-03T15:23+10:00). *Guidance on Therapeutic Goods (Conformity Assessment Standard for Quality Management Systems) Order 2019.* https://www.tga.gov.au/guidance-therapeutic-goods-conformity-assessment-standard-quality-management-systems-order-2019

United Nations - Department of Economic and Social Affairs. *The 17 Goals*. United Nations - Department of Economic and Social Affairs. https://sdgs.un.org/goals

United Nations. (2011). *Guiding Principles On Business and Human Rights*. United Nations. https://www.ohchr.org/sites/default/files/Documents/Publications/GuidingPrinciplesBusinessHR_EN.pdf

Venkateswara Rao, T. (2016). *Performance management : towards organizational excellence* (2nd ed.). SAGE Publications India Pvt Ltd.

Victoria. (2024a). *How a law is made*. Parliament of Victoria. https://www.parliament.vic.gov.au/

Victoria. (2024b). *Victorian courts and tribunals*. Victoria. https://courts.vic.gov.au/court-system/victorian-courts-and-tribunals

Watt v Hertfordshire County Council [1954] EWCA 6. http://www.bailii.org/ew/cases/EWCA/Civ/1954/6.html

Western Australia. (2024a). *Court System in Western Australia*. Western Australia,. https://www.supremecourt.wa.gov.au/

Western Australia. (2024b). *The Legislative Process*. Parliament of Western Australia. https://www.parliament.wa.gov.au/

Wilsons & Clyde Coal Co v English [1938] AC 57. https://www.bailii.org/

Work Health and Safety (General) Regulations 2022. (W.A.).

Work Health and Safety Act 2011. (Austl.).

Work Health and Safety Act 2020. (W.A.).

Work Health and Safety Regulations 2011. (Austl.).

Worksafe (ACT). (2020, 2020-10-01 09:04:26). *Record keeping - WorkSafe ACT*. https://www.worksafe.act.gov.au/health-and-safety-portal/managing-safety/record-keeping

Worksafe (ACT). (2024). *Legislation*. Australian Capital Territory. https://www.worksafe.act.gov.au/

Worksafe (NT). (2024). *Laws and compliance*. Northern Territory. https://worksafe.nt.gov.au/

Worksafe (Qld). (2020). Consultation, representation and participation. Retrieved 2020-06-26 12:00:09, from https://www.worksafe.qld.gov.au/laws-and-compliance/work-health-and-safety-laws/consultation-representation-and-participation

Worksafe (Qld). (2024). *Work Health and Safety Laws*. Queensland. https://www.worksafe.qld.gov.au/

Worksafe (TAS). (2024). *Acts and Regulations*. Tasmania. https://worksafe.tas.gov.au/

Worksafe (Vic). (2017). *Safe handling of industrial waste*. Worksafe (Vic) Retrieved from https://content-v2.api.worksafe.vic.gov.au/sites/default/files/2018-06/ISBN-Safe-handling-of-industrial-waste-guide-2013-05.pdf

Worksafe (VIC). (2024). *All Acts and Regulations*. Victoria. https://www.worksafe.vic.gov.au/

Worksafe (WA). (2023). *Interpretive Guideline Incident Notification*. Retrieved from https://www.wa.gov.au/system/files/2023-02/231149_GL_IncidentNotification.pdf

World Health Organisation. (2024). *Mental health at work*. United Nations. https://www.who.int/news-room/fact-sheets/detail/mental-health-at-work

Index of terms

Tim Damianidis

www.ingramcontent.com/pod-product-compliance
Lightning Source LLC
Chambersburg PA
CBHW070325270326
41926CB00017B/3762